MW00799938

RETIRE EARLY
RETIRE WELL

The No Nonsense Guide To Million Dollar
Wealth Building Alternatives

M.C. Keithley

INVESMART PUBLISHERS
EL CAJON, CA

Quantity orders of this book are available at substantial discounts. For information contact Customer Service Department, (800) 247-6553.

Text is printed on acid-free paper.

Published by Invesmart Publishers
1265 Avocado Blvd., Suite 104-225, El Cajon, California 92020-7704.

Library of Congress Catalog Card Number: 97-094984

Keithley, M. C.
Retire early, retire well: the no nonsense guide to million dollar wealth building alternatives/M. C. Keithley

ISBN: 0-9654186-0-X
    p.   cm.

Includes bibliography/works cited, other resources, and index.

1.   Finance, Personal   2.   Retirement Income-United States-Planning
3.   Investment Analysis

Dedication

To those beginning and seasoned investors who seek the safest and fastest route to financial independence or early retirement — not to be detoured by the "Wealth Busters."

Especially to investors determined to select for themselves from only proven investments and strategies — those that realistically could lead to a million dollars at retirement.

TABLE OF CONTENTS

Acknowledgments

To Betty, my wife, whose positive influence in everything I've attempted has made a huge difference. As best friend, business partner, and wonderful mother of our four children her support has been invaluable.

To our children, Scott, Susanne, Robert and Laura for their love and understanding, especially in the early years when money was scarce and yet we enjoyed some of our most precious times together.

During the year and one-half that it took to research and write this book, it occurred to me how indebted we are to past author/entrepreneurs who chose to share their insights and success with us. Without such mentors, mastering the techniques of successful investing would certainly be a more formidable task for all of us.

In order to get a book into print, the grammar, spelling, structure and organization must be critiqued. Penny Munroe served admirably in her capacity of editor/technical assistant, insuring that the needs of the reader and the publisher were both met. A special thanks to Bonnie Brunson and her considerable data processing skills, she could always be relied upon to meet demanding publisher/printer deadlines.

I will be forever grateful to the first agent that took an interest in my book. It was Dr. Albert Halff of the Blake Group, he saw a potential "best seller" in my work, and it was his encouragement that eventually brought about publication.

Although each of us is responsible for our own success, I believe the confidence we gain in being able to share the success of others who have preceded us, is critical. Knowing that what is presented here is not just my knowledge, but the product of many successful people who have helped shape my own success over some 35 years of investing; it is my hope that the confidence gained will lead to your own early success in investing and ultimately, if you wish, to the benefits of early retirement.

PREFACE
Where I'm Coming From

As a teenager growing up in Omaha, Nebraska in the late forties and early fifties, I recall my father and grandfather reminiscing about the difficult times of the Great Depression of the 1930s. They spoke of what a challenge it had been for most people to just put food on the table and keep a roof over their head. It was commonplace for several families to move in together to save on rent and to pool their funds in order to buy food and fuel. Jobs were almost impossible to get because thousands of men, unemployed like my father, had no more than a seventh or eighth grade education.

Eventually, through a friend, my father found work at the smelters tending the blast furnaces. However, after a few weeks, he severely injured his foot in an accident and again he was unable to support our family. At this point, in order to make ends meet, my mother had to take work as a house-keeper and baby-sitter for a wealthy family.

Several years later things did begin to improve for me, my sister and two brothers. The only difficulty came from the frequent moves my family was forced to make in order to supplement his wages. Every two to four years, my father would sell our home, buy another fixer-upper and then repeat the process.

It was from this background and the need to work part-time throughout high school that I learned the value of money and the security and independence that it provided. Later, as an enlisted man in the Navy earning $90 per month, I not only learned to stretch my pay from one monthly pay-check to the next, but also to save and invest a small percentage regularly.

After nearly three years in the Navy, I was finally able to buy my first car. After my discharge and with the help of the G.I. Bill, part-time work plus my new bride's assistance, I was able to enter and eventually complete a four-year college program at San Diego State University. It had been my dream to graduate to a high paying career and earn the income needed to create comfort and security for myself and family.

My career in personnel progressed steadily for several years until I realized that working for wages alone would be insufficient. I wanted an income that would allow me to live well and create the level of security and independence that I craved and the means to retire early if I chose to do so. Soon thereafter I became the owner of my first business, an employment agency.

An avid reader, I had read many books on self improvement and acquiring wealth, but it wasn't until I read William Nickerson's book: <u>How I Turned $1,000 into a Million in Real Estate — In My Spare Time</u> that I was finally moved to action. Soon after, my wife and I purchased our first of many rental properties to come.

Several years later I found the business that I enjoyed the most and the one that turned out to be the most profitable. After a year of producing outstanding results for this company as an employee, I was offered the opportunity to buy into the company. I negotiated a buy-out with the owner that allowed me to buy the business on a pay as you go basis, from future profits. For the next 14 years I was president and majority stockholder of a medium sized construction company and eventually a consultant to the industry. Five years ago I sold a majority of my stock and assumed a supportive role in order to travel, enjoy retirement and pursue other interests— including the writing of this book.

During those years that I was operating the

business, we were also expanding our apartment holdings. However, as profits from the business continued to grow, it forced me to become an astute investor of these excess funds. I also became an astute investor of the excess funds generated by the apartments. This required searching out and investigating a wide range of investment possibilities. In addition, during this time our small company pension had grown to over one-half million dollars, and early on it had become my responsibility to manage and invest these funds as well. The range of this investment exposure was broad: everything from stocks, bonds and warrants, to gold and silver and options. These investments also ranged from limited partnership oil wells to houseboats on Lake Shasta and from newer products such as GNMAs and low income housing to variable annuities and zero coupon bonds. One of the valuable lessons that I learned very quickly was that some of these products were designed mainly for tax benefits, some for solid returns, while others were pure speculations.

As you can well imagine, during this trial and error period, I made some mistakes. In spite of having no one to guide me, I learned from my mistakes, the company and pension accounts continued to grow, and my own personal net worth also grew — into the millions.

My good fortune allowed me to retire in my midfifties, to travel extensively, and to indulge my interests in hunting, fishing and golf. Most importantly, I gained the financial independence to provide well for my family — free of the insecurity I had known as a youngster — and even to insure the well being and education of my grandchildren.

It is my intention to share with you the investment knowledge that I have gained in over thirty years of successful investing for myself and others. I will explain the same low risk methods that I have employed and the same successful investments that I invest in myself.

Finally, it is my hope that by avoiding the ups and downs that were a necessary part of my own learning process, your personal wealth building efforts will be more quickly rewarded. Beginning with the first chapter, you will learn the most important factor in building wealth. This knowledge alone, applied correctly, can multiply your own wealth night and day, 24 hours a day, 7 days a week.

Introduction
Investing —
the Best Alternatives

According to a recent study conducted by the brokerage firm Merrill Lynch & Co., people in the 25 to 44 age bracket are saving at a rate that will provide them with less than a third of what they will need to maintain their current lifestyle when they retire. The reality of this finding is reflected in the frustration of the typical person one might talk to in this age group. Most say their earnings are up, but so are their taxes and the cost of the new car they need and the house they would like to buy.

Coupled with this problem is the low rate of interest they are able to earn on the limited amount of funds they are able to set aside in their bank or money account. This is further complicated by the fact that "The average investor is excessively cautious. Too much of the money naps in fixed-interest vehicles. Not enough is invested in stocks for growth." This is according to syndicated national financial columnist, Jane Bryant Quinn (D-4).

Overcoming these problems can be as simple as starting the right kind of small investment program as soon as possible. However, the information on how to get started and the various options can be confusing and sometimes contradictory as we are bombarded with a mass of financial information from the press and various publications. Clear and specific information will be presented and fully explained in the chapters which follow.

Although the amount that the IRS takes out of our paychecks is somewhat (but not entirely) out of our control, I will outline a number of strategies which you can use to create investment funds from expenditures that you now make. This spending can be modified, or come from sources that you may have forgotten that you have.

All the principal investments that will be recommended in this book will share these common characteristics:

1. Tax advantaged or tax sheltered. Investments that the IRS favors in such a way as to reduce your personal income tax or defer taxes indefinitely. The less taxes you pay, the more rapidly your investments will grow.

2.   Inflation hedged or even inflation advantaged.

3.   High rates of return with relatively low risk.

4.   The safe use of leverage will be employed to increase the rate of return.

5.   How to buy below market value will be employed as another strategy to increase return.

These investments will be further distinguished by their exceptional profitability, the ease with which these profits can be multiplied, and the safety of principal.

Regardless of whether you are an experienced investor or just starting out, if you are in your 20s or even in your 50s, and looking for the right wealth building plan, I believe that the investments profiled in this book will give you the confidence to successfully provide for your future.

This book is unique in that it combines the presentation of investments as diverse as stocks and bonds, real estate of various kinds and even a business of your own. It is one that compares each investment against the other, without the typical bias for the stock market. I would like to assure you that every investment I recommend in this book, I have invested in myself. They're very profitable, and for my money are "the cream of the crop". Of course there are many "get rich quick" schemes that promise even more, but the vast majority simply don't work, or if they work at all, fall far short of the extravagant claims made to entice you. Don't waste your money.

Most of these "get rich quick" schemes are not investments at all, but are pure speculation. Examples would be: "If the price of gold goes to $600 . . ." or "If we strike oil as we expect . . ." or "If you act now you can earn 1,000% on your investment in the next six months . . ." These are all very big ifs.

More difficult to ignore are our own brokers, sometimes pitching stocks that are "poised for a major run-up" (stocks that are already overpriced) or (for a new and unproven issue) "a can't miss stock that's due to double." These are dubious claims at best or shamelessly self serving at worst.

One final note. I will make frequent reference to certain books, newsletters and specific products or services by name that I have found to be particularly helpful. These are outstanding for the purpose of providing you with supplemental information in your pursuit of the investments in this book. Be assured that I have no financial interest in any of these publications, products or services, and receive absolutely nothing for making these recommendations. My sole motivation is to steer you to as many sources as I can that have been helpful or profitable to me — sources that I believe will help you to reach your own wealth building goals sooner. And, if you wish, help you to achieve an early, comfortable retirement.

PART I: FORMULA FOR WEALTH

Chapter 1: Millionaire's Secret

What is it that allows one person to become wealthy, while others, seemingly just as smart and industrious, fall short? Of course there can be many reasons: lack of motivation, failure to save, poor selection of investment alternatives, or just simply inconsistency in investment habits and not investing for the long term.

Assuming that wealthy investors have none of these afflictions, the chances are that there is one underlying dynamic that nearly all wealthy investors employ — knowingly or not — that virtually assures their investment success. The same dynamic utilized by every major bank, insurance company, and virtually all financial institutions. Their secret and the millionaire's secret is that dynamic of money-making known as compound interest. This "magic of compounding," as applied to stocks, real estate or your own business, is the single most important element at work in the investment alternatives presented. It can — in time — build great wealth.

Let's take a look at the rather spectacular results that compounding can produce. **[See Figure 1]** In

Retire Early, Retire Well

FIGURE 1 - EARLY START IRA[1]

	INVESTOR A		INVESTOR B	
Age	Contribution	Year-end value	Contribution	Year-end value
19			2,000	2,200
20			2,000	4,620
21			2,000	7,282
22			2,000	10,210
23			2,000	13,341
24			2,000	16,974
25			2,000	20,872
26	2,000	2,200	-0-	22,959
27	2,000	4,620	-0-	25,255
28	2,000	7,282	-0-	27,780
29	2,000	10,210	-0-	30,588
30	2,000	13,431	-0-	33,614
31	2,000	16,974	-0-	36,974
32	2,000	20,872	-0-	40,673
33	2,000	25,159	-0-	44,741
34	2,000	29,875	-0-	49,215
35	2,000	35,062	-0-	54,136
36	2,000	40,769	-0-	59,550
37	2,000	47,045	-0-	65,505
38	2,000	53,950	-0-	72,055
39	2,000	61,545	-0-	79,261
40	2,000	69,899	-0-	87,187
41	2,000	79,089	-0-	95,905
42	2,000	89,198	-0-	105,496
43	2,000	100,318	-0-	116,045
44	2,000	112,550	-0-	127,650
45	2,000	126,005	-0-	140,415
46	2,000	140,805	-0-	154,456
47	2,000	157,086	-0-	169,902
48	2,000	174,995	-0-	186,892
49	2,000	194,694	-0-	205,581
50	2,000	216,364	-0-	226,140
51	2,000	240,200	-0-	248,754
52	2,000	266,420	-0-	273,629
53	2,000	295,262	-0-	300,992
54	2,000	326,988	-0-	331,091
55	2,000	361,887	-0-	364,200
56	2,000	400,276	-0-	400,620
57	2,000	442,503	-0-	440,682
58	2,000	488,953	-0-	484,750
59	2,000	540,049	-0-	533,225
60	2,000	596,254	-0-	586,548
61	2,000	658,079	-0-	645,203
62	2,000	726,087·	-0-	709,723
63	2,000	800,896	-0-	780,695
64	2,000	883,185	-0-	858,765
65	2,000	973,704	-0-	944,641
Less Total Invested	(80,000)		(14,000)	
Equals Net Earnings:	893,704		930,641	
Money Grew	11-fold		66-fold	

---

[1]*Market Logic*, Glen King Parker, Publisher. Reprinted by permission.

30

Figure 1 we assume that Investor B is a 19 year old who invests $2,000 each year until his 25th birthday. At that time he gets married, starts a family and is unable to make additional contributions thereafter. Assuming an investment rate of return of 10%, in an IRA account with tax-free compounding of earnings and all earnings reinvested, at the time of his retirement at age 65, he will have net earnings of $930,641. Not bad for an initial investment of only $14,000.

On the other hand, Investor A starts his investment program seven years later at age 26 and continues to add an additional $2,000 per year until age 65. Even though he contributes considerably more (a total of $80,000), his net earnings, though impressive, of $893,704 are somewhat less than Investor B.

The lesson here is clear: <u>The earlier in life you begin an investment program and the more years you allow the investment to compound, the greater your return will be.</u>
In order to get the benefit of an entirely different scenario, let's assume an Investor C's employer decides to discontinue the company's 401(k) pension plan (an all too frequent trend these days). At age 32 he's

been with the company for 10 years and is fully vested with an accumulation of $20,000 based on matching contributions made by the employee and employer. Dissatisfied with this turn of events, Investor C changes jobs and does a rollover to his new employer's pension plan, which allows employees to manage their own funds (a favorable trend these days). The employee selects mutual funds and with the use of techniques like those used in this book, manages a return of 15% annually, compounded monthly. In addition, he signs up for a payroll deduction of $100 per month in order to be able to add to his plan on a monthly basis. **[See Figure 2]** Figure 2 illustrates how compounding at 15% will work in this scenario with an initial investment of $20,000 and an additional investment of $100 monthly thereafter until early retirement at age 62. Here again the results are impressive. Investor C will have $1,885,092 at retirement.

Another lesson to be learned: <u>Small amounts added regularly to an investment that is allowed to compound over a considerable period of time will improve results dramatically, as will a higher rate of return (i.e. 15% vs 10%).</u>

Once you've made the commitment to put the power of compounding to work for you, your choice of one or more investment vehicles becomes critical.

FIGURE 2 - INVESTOR C[2]

Age	Investment	Monthly $100	End Year
32	Initial amount: $ 20,000	$ 1,286	1
37	40,228	8,730	5
42	80,912	26,273	10
47	162,742	61,528	15
52	327,330	132,375	20
57	658,378	274,747	25
62	1,324,234	560,856	30
Investment + Monthly = TOTAL $1,885,092			

[2]"How to be Your Own Investment Counselor," *Telephone Switch Newsletter*, Publisher, P.O. Box 2538, Huntington Beach, CA 92647

Should that investment underperform or fail, the results can seriously cripple your ability to reach your wealth building goal. On the other hand, should you select an investment vehicle that exceeds the targeted rate of return of 10% to 15%, one of two things is likely to happen. Either you will reach your goal years earlier than planned or you will accumulate far greater wealth than you had anticipated or thought possible.

Because this choice of vehicles is so important, only vehicles that you have a comfort level with should be selected. In choosing one, you should know what rate of return you can reasonably expect from each. Because investment alternatives are seldom presented in this manner and because relative rates of return from these types of investments are rarely compared, I will spend the better part of this book giving you the kind of information that you will need in order to evaluate and then select from the many investment alternatives presented.

<u>Key Points</u>: The real secret, then, to accumulating substantial wealth or becoming a millionaire, is to invest like a millionaire. This involves taking the long term approach, seeking above average rates of return coupled with safety of principal, and allowing the powerful forces of compounding to multiply your investment.

PART II: STOCKS

Chapter 2: Major Holding of The Wealthy — A Perspective

A recent study of the wealthiest families in America found the highest percentage of their wealth to be invested in the stock market. Surprisingly, these holdings even exceeded the value of their holdings in real estate. This finding is less of a surprise when the statistics compiled over the past 30 years are considered: The compound annual rate of return for stocks is 9.83% compared to a lesser return of 8.46% for commercial real estate according to a study by Ibbotson Associates, 1991. If we are to conclude from this that the wealth building possibilities of investing in the stock market are worth considering, then a look at the past 20 years is even more revealing.

If you had invested $1,000 twenty years ago in the 30 Dow stocks that make up the Dow Jones Industrial Average, your stock would have been worth only $1,731 after 10 years or $7,954 after 20 years. And yet, if you had used a simple, effective system that is now available, using just a five-stock strategy, starting with the same $1,000 you could have realized $6,212 after 10 years or $42,305 after 20 years. That works out to an average return over the 20 years of over $2,000 per year on the original investment of

$1,000. This is the O'Higgins Dow Beating System, one of several excellent systems that we will explore in the following chapters.

My belief is that anyone can invest successfully in the stock market, as long as they follow a few basic guidelines, are patient, and have a definite plan of investment or system that they will consistently adhere to. In order to increase your profits and maximize the effect of compounding, it is important that stocks be held in a tax deferred vehicle such as an IRA, company pension plan or variable annuity so that no taxes will be due until you start withdrawals at some future date.

Since the historical returns from the stock market in this century have averaged about 10% total return annually, and a little less than half of that return is based on dividends, most of the investment plans or systems that will be covered will stress utilizing dividends as well as growth, in order to insure the steady increase in the value of our stock portfolios, and to decrease risk.

Key Points: The investment habits of the wealthy and the long term statistics of the stock market tell us that this can be a key area of wealth accumulation, provided we have a definite plan or system which we will consistently follow.

Chapter 3: Mutual Funds — Keeping it Simple

"Mutual funds could be considered the ultimate compounding vehicle. Nowhere else has an investment vehicle taken more advantage of the principles of compounding and the use of reinvestment dividends to further enhance its returns."

*- from **Jim Blanchard's High Yield Newsletter***

Due to the consistent profitability of many mutual funds, especially those relying on growth and dividends, there has been a tremendous interest in mutual funds which has continued to grow for nearly two decades now - a period which has been primarily a bull market. As interest rates have dropped over the last several years, the move out of bank CDs, money market accounts and bonds has accelerated, with stocks and mutual funds becoming the biggest beneficiary. This massive move into stocks is easily understood if one compares the cumulative investment returns and inflation as illustrated in Figure 3. **[See Figure 3]**

Figure 3

CUMULATIVE INVESTMENT RETURNS AND INFLATION
Periods Ended 12/31/91[3]

	Years			
	5	10	15	20
Stocks (S&P 500)	104%	406%	646%	848%
Bonds - Government	60	325	303	460
Bonds - Corporate	64	352	324	507
Treasury Bills	38	109	232	342
Inflation (CPI)	25	47	137	236

---

[3] Ibbotson Associates

Take, for example, column three. We see for the last 15 years that stocks (Standard & Poor's 500) returned 646%, nearly double that of bonds, almost triple that of T-bills, and more than quadruple the accumulated inflation rate. What better reason, then, for us to examine mutual funds.

A mutual fund is a single group of stocks held within a fund for diversification with a manager to provide professional management. Unfortunately, what was intended as a simple way to invest in the stock market, has expanded from the original handful of funds to more than 3,000 mutual funds. This is more than twice as many funds as there are stocks on the New York Stock Exchange. This overwhelming number of funds, coupled with the fact that only 18% of the mutual funds beat the S&P 500 over the last 10 years (Lipper Analytical Services, 1993), suggests that a simpler approach is needed.

That brings us to the only remaining simplified approach to mutual funds: Index Funds. These funds are designed to reflect certain market averages such as the S&P 500, or the Russell 2000. These are the best known indexes beyond the Dow Jones Industrial Average, which is composed of just 30 stocks. The

S&P 500 index is a measurement of the average performance of 500 of the most commonly held stocks on the New York Stock Exchange, the American Stock Exchange, and the NASDAQ small stock over-the-counter market, and this performance is based on total return, including growth and dividends. On the other hand, the Russell 2000 reflects the performance of 2,000 of the smallest stocks in the Russell 3000, this index typically includes little or no dividend return from most of these small stocks.

The best of these for our purposes is the Vanguard Index 500 fund, a no-load fund. This means that no commission is charged to buy this fund. It has the longest track record of these types of funds and its annual fees are among the lowest in the industry. Also, this fund group includes many other good funds, including one of the highest paying money market funds, Vanguard Prime. This group of funds is popular because of the wide range of funds available and their reputation for low administrative costs. Lower administrative cost increases your net return.

The Vanguard Index 500 reflects the over-all performance of the market. That record shows an average return of 13.5% for 1986-1990, with a high of 18% for 1986 and a low of -3% for 1990. For the five year period ending 9/3/93 the fund was up 104% or an average of 20.8% per year. This is a "one decision," purely mechanical investment that allows you to "buy and hold" without the need for the fund manager to buy or sell the right stocks at the right time.

These statistics are from the <u>Mutual Fund Forecaster</u> (2) newsletter.

The other important aspect of this investment is the modest risk. With the diversification of 500 stocks and the added stability of stocks that have the largest capitalization, you have an investment with much less volatility.

There are about a dozen index funds that are similar to the Vanguard Index 500, most of which have been in existence for less than ten years. Despite this, Vanguard has the best five and ten year total return (14.9% annually to 3/31/91) of all these funds. (As of 12/31/96, still 14.99% annually.)

You can buy this fund directly from Vanguard without any fee or from discount brokers who charge a small transaction fee — as little as $27.

Vanguard Fund - Index 500   Toll Free: 800-662-7447

Discounters:
Aufhauser & Co 800-368-3668
Jack White 800-233-3411
Fidelity 800-225-1799
Charles Schwab 800-435-4000

Key Points: This Index Fund can keep an investment in stocks, or equities, simple and conservative.   One can take advantage of the appreciation and dividends that can be realized and accumulated, with no effort. By utilizing a "no-load" fund and a discount broker, you can keep your costs low and be able to invest in the simplest and most convenient way.

Chapter 4: Buy and Hold, or Switch?

In the preceding chapter, I think we made a compelling case for index mutual funds. However, since the level of risk with various other funds ranges from very low too very high, a strong case can be made for a "switch strategy" for the funds at the higher risk levels.

What is a "switch" strategy, and why would we consider buying the higher risk funds? The "switch strategy" is one that was developed by Dick Fabian, editor of the Telephone Switch Newsletter, which has been directing its readers' investment selections and "timing the market" for more than 18 years. The strategy involves buying from a group of typically 20 to 30 recommended funds when a buy signal is issued from the newsletter, switching out of those funds into a money market fund when a sell signal is given, and switching back into better performing funds when the buy signal is issued again. Switching is done with a single phone call.

The recommended funds invariably include many medium to very high risk funds — included because of their superior performance during certain time frames. The strategy here is to maximize your return while you are invested in mutual fund equities in a generally rising market then minimize your downside risk by switching into no risk money market funds during times when the market is trending down. The higher risk funds offer potentially higher returns to your mutual fund portfolio in the overall strategy. At the heart of this strategy is the 39 week market averages of the Mutual Fund Composite and the Dow Jones 65 Composite. The newsletter keeps track of both of these for you and issues "alerts" when either of these averages drops 5% below their 39 week averages.

The results of this strategy are impressive. The actual growth realized by this strategy was approximately 18% since inception of the newsletter in 1977. An investment of $10,000 then would be worth $95,439 14 years later. Using this strategy, a 32-year-old who starts with $10,000, at age 62 will have accumulated $1,433,706. Or, let's take hypothetical Investor D. **[See Figure 4]** He doesn't get around to starting a serious investment program until age 40. At that time, he also starts with a $10,000 investment and invests an additional $100 per month until retirement at age 65. He will have accumulated $1,078,080.

FIGURE 4 - INVESTOR D
Compounding rate 18%

Age	Investment	Monthly $100	End Year
40	Initial amt: $ 10,000	$ 1,304	1
45	22,877	9,405	5
50	52,338	30,935	10
55	119,737	80,225	15
60	273,930	193,065	20
65	626,686	451,394	25
Investment + Monthly = Total $1,078,080			

Fabian's <u>Telephone Switch Newsletter</u>, (recently changed names to <u>Fabian's Investment Resource</u>) achieves the results it does with a selection of five mutual funds that make up the Mutual Fund Composite. Two of my favorite, very high risk funds are the Columbia Special and the Twentieth Century Ultra Funds. They have five-year annual average returns of 19.19% and 22.42% respectively (as of 7/31/97). These funds are included in the Mutual Fund Composite from time to time and can be ideal for generally rising markets. They yield superior results as long as they are sold when a sell signal is given of impending bear market. Because of their volatility, they can be up more than 50% (1991) and down more than 12% (1990) in the case of Columbia, or up more than 86% (1991) and down more than 19% (1984) in the case of Ultra.

Two other funds, suitable for either a "switch" strategy or a "buy and hold" strategy, are the low risk fund, Invesco (formerly Financial) Industrial Income Fund and the medium risk Janus Fund. Industrial income (five year return as of 7/31/97, 16.44%) has not had a negative year in more than 12 years and even in the tough major market drop year of 1987, came through with a 4.9% return. Also, I like its conservative investment policy of investing for a high yield with some capital appreciation.

Janus, (five year return as of 7/31/97, 17.40%) on the other hand, has an investment policy of investing for long term growth and diversifying its portfolio among large and small companies. This has allowed them to have some exceptional years like a gain of 46% in 1989 and 42% in 1991. There were only two down years in the last 12 years — and both years recorded less than a 1% loss. This is the type of steady performance that will allow compounding to work year after year.

If you would like more information on Fabian's newsletter and strategy contact:

Fabian's Investment Resource
P.O. Box 2538 Huntington Beach, Ca. 92647
Phone 1-800-391-1118
Published monthly. Subscription: 1 year $137.

If you would like a prospectus, or to order any of these funds, you may contact the funds themselves or contact one of the discount brokers listed in the Appendix.

In order to further evaluate these funds, or to compare their records with other funds, I would suggest contacting the major library in your area in order to review one or more of these four publications which are published annually or more frequently:

Mutual Funds Panorama, CDA/Wiesenberger
Morningstar Mutual, Morningstar, Inc.
Mutual Fund Profiles, Standard & Poors/Lipper
No-Load Mutual Funds, American Associate Individual
    Investors

In addition, if you wish to know more about all major funds, their risk rating and their profit projections for the next one-year and five-year periods, the Mutual Fund Forecaster provides such information and is an excellent newsletter. For information call 1-800-442-9000. Subscriptions to this monthly newsletter are $100 per year.

Key Point: Deciding when to buy a fund and when to sell it are the toughest and most critical calls a person will have to make as a mutual fund investor. If you decide to follow Fabian's strategy, these will be easy decisions as it will become automatic to respond to the buy and sell signals as given. He will identify the best funds for you to select from, most of which will have had the best record of performance over at least the last five or ten years. In addition, Fabian gives you their current performance in every issue, and then recommends those funds that performed best in the last switch cycle. In order for you to get the best results from compounding, avoiding loss becomes every bit as important as achieving above average returns for your funds. This is where Fabian's strategy shines, he not only makes it possible, he makes it likely. Not only that, you sleep well nights — whether the stock market is going up or down.

Chapter 5: Beat the Dow!

"O'Higgins picks only from the 30 stocks in the Dow Jones Industrial Average . . . and his performance over the last three years placed him in the top one percent of all U.S. money managers."

Louis Rukeyser, _Wall Street Week_

Before we look at "O'Higgins systems," we need to consider the fact that most investors who fail, do so due to the lack of a comprehensive plan. Buying individual stocks can be a complex and frustrating experience for most investors. They see the financial headlines where some new "hot stock" is up 50 percent in just 30 days, or one of Wall Street's gurus like Peter Lynch in his book One Up on Wall Street, is claiming an expected gain of 30 to 50 percent from his investment in big company "stalwarts," and much more from the "fast growers." This makes it appear to be easy to make big money in stocks, leading many investors without a specific game plan to buy popular but over priced stocks at market highs, only to sell these same stocks at a loss on any disappointing news or market downturn.

The fact is, as we learned earlier, that even the professional money managers of mutual funds beat the market averages on a regular basis less than half the time. This is why I think <u>Beating the Dow</u>, written by Michael O'Higgins, offers the average investor a terrific and simple system for beating the averages. Since most investors have neither the time nor the patience to do the necessary research or to follow more complicated systems, this system offers them the opportunity to realize substantial profits with a once a year decision. Due to the minimum time that I choose to spend on my own stock investments, this is one of the systems that I employ personally.

In order to understand this system, you need to know that it is based on a low risk approach to the market which takes advantage of the high yields, or dividends, of some of the largest and most successful companies in the U.S. These stocks necessarily come from the 30 stocks that make up the Dow Jones industrial average. Then only ten of these high yield stocks, those with the lowest prices, are considered. The consistent profitability of this system is not at all surprising if you consider that it is based on two readily available historical facts of the market: (1) over long periods of time, nearly half the gains in the market come from dividends; and (2 there is a tendency for less expensive stocks to move in greater percentage increments than higher priced stocks. These facts, coupled with a tendency for the lowest priced stocks in the Dow to be artificially low, because their companies are temporarily out of favor, almost assure the investor's success. The rebound of these "blue chip" companies is likely due to their tremendous financial strength and resources, which typically allow them to overcome their problems. The result is that they return to higher levels of profitability and as a consequence, to higher stock price levels.

The best way to quickly grasp this system and its potential is to examine the five-stock and ten-stock selections for the 1992 year and the total return results for each as shown in Figure 5. **[See Figure 5]**

As you can see, the five-stock portfolio that includes Westinghouse at the lowest beginning price, $17.88, Sears at $37.88 the highest, ended the 1992 year up 23.22%, versus the Dow Jones Industrial Average for all 30 stocks of just 7.44%. The much more conservative ten-stock portfolio, beginning with the highest yielding Westinghouse with a yield of 7.83% and ending with IBM yielding 5.44%, still managed to beat the Dow with a 7.92% total return.

FIGURE 5[4]

FULL YEAR 1992 RESULTS					
12/31/91 10 Highest Yields	Stocks (in order of low to high price)	12/31/91 Price	12/31/92 Price	Total Return	Portfolio Average
7.83%	Westinghouse	17.88	13.25	--- 21.85%	
4.94	Union Carbide	20.25	33.38	69.78*	
4.91	American Express	20.38	24.88	26.99	
5.54	General Motors	28.88	32.13	16.10	
5.28	Sears	37.88	45.38	25.08	23.22%
4.15	Eastman Kodak	48.25	40.50	11.92	
4.40	Exxon	60.88	61.13	4.98	
5.21	Texaco	61.38	59.75	2.57	
4.78	Chevron	60.00	69.50	5.51	
5.44	IBM	89.00	50.38	--- 37.96	7.92%

Dow Jones Industrial Average: 3168.83   3301.11   7.44%
*Penultimate Profit Prospect (Inclides Praxair @ 16.75)

[4]Beating the Dow, January 1993, Vol. 1, No. 1, The Hirsch Organization. Reprinted by permission.

To put this in perspective, we need to see what the results have actually been from an investment in the five-stock high yield/low price strategy over the past 20 years. **[See Figure 6]** In Figure 6, we can see that whereas a $1,000 investment in the 30 stock Dow grew to a respectable $7,964, the five-stock strategy grew to $42,305 — a tremendous wealth building difference. Of course there is technically more risk in a five-stock portfolio than in a 30-stock portfolio of all the Dow stocks. However, the results over 20 years tells a different story. In the five-stock strategy we can see that there were only two negative return years, 1974 and 1990, both very poor years for the stock market in general. On the other hand, in the Actual Dow, there were five negative return years: 1973, 1974, 1977, 1981, and 1990. Also, it is interesting to note that the size of the biggest loss in the Actual Dow was larger at 23.14% than the largest loss in the five-stock strategy at 15.22%.

For my money, I would rather be in the five or ten- stock strategy. Most investors cannot afford to own all 30 stocks in the Dow. Since I think the risk in the five or ten-stock strategy is reduced due to the fact that you are typically buying these stocks at the low of their price range, and their high yields tend to act as a further brake against big price drops, I believe all but the most conservative of investors can safely

FIGURE 6[5]

	Five Stock Strategy	What the Dow Did	In Five Stock Strategy	In the Actual Dow
1973	19.64%	---13.12%	$ 1,196	$ 868
1974	---3.75	---23.14	1,151	667
1975	70.07	44.40	1,958	964
1976	40.79	22.72	2,757	1,183
1977	4.47	---12.71	2,880	1,033
1978	1.65	2.69	2,298	1,060
1979	9.91	10.52	3,218	1,173
1980	40.53	21.41	4,522	1,424
1981	0.01	---3.40	4,522	1,376
1982	37.36	25.79	6,212	1,731
1983	36.11	25.65	8,456	2,175
1984	12.64	1.08	9,525	2,198
1985	37.83	32.78	13,128	2,919
1986	27.90	26.92	16,791	3,705
1987	11.06	6.05	18,648	3,928
1988	21.43	15.95	22,644	4,554
1989	10.49	31.71	25,020	5,999
1990	---15.22	---0.40	21,212	5,975
1991	61.86	23.91	34,333	7,403
1992	23.22	7.44	$42,305	$7,954

[5]Beating the Dow, January 1993, Vol. 1, No. 1, The Hirsch

Organization. Reprinted by permission.

own these shares. This allows them to realize the significantly higher total returns with relative safety — returns that are otherwise unlikely if they were to pick stocks on their own.

The results of the five-stock strategy over the 20-year period illustrated in Figure 6 works out to a compounding rate of 20.5%, (21.1% as of 1/1/97). If we round this off to 20%, and use the same example as we did in Chapter 4, we can illustrate the results in Figure 7, as Investor E. The tremendous difference in having a 20% compound rate working for you versus the 18% illustrated in Figure 4, Chapter 4, reveals a difference of $602,081 in value at the end of this period. ($1,579,920 versus $1,078,080). An accumulated return of nearly 50% more entirely due to 2% greater rate of compounding of the investment. **[See Figure 7]**

This concept is so sound, so simple, and so saleable to the public that even the big brokerage firms such as Dean Witter Reynolds and Merrill Lynch have jumped on the "band wagon." Their version is to package a group of ten high yielding blue chip stocks in something called a unit trust, charge you a fee of approximately 2% to 4% to get in and an annual reinvestment/management fee of 1% to 2%. In just the last year, this concept proved so popular that they

FIGURE 7 - INVESTOR E
Compounding Rate 20%

Age	Investment	Monthly $100	End Year
40	Initial amt: $ 10,000	$ 1,316	1
45	24,833	9,870	5
50	61,917	34,430	10
55	154,070	95,540	15
60	383,375	247,599	20
65	953,962	625,958	25
Investment + Monthly = TOTAL $1,579,920			

sold hundreds of millions of dollars of this product. Fortunately for you, you can avail yourself of a similar product with a longer track record without any fees other than the cost of the broker's commission to buy the stock, and if you utilize a discount broker or negotiate a discount commission with a full service broker, even this fee can be small.

All 30 stocks comprising the Dow are regularly listed in the Wall Street Journal under The Dow Jones Averages and subtitled: "30 Stocks In Industrial Average — NYSE." At the beginning of 1992 you could have bought 100 shares of all five of the lowest priced stocks with the highest yields, for $12,527 — plus commissions and sold at the end of the year for $14,902 including dividends paid less commissions, approximately a 19% gain. This was during a time when money market accounts were paying typically only 3.5% to 4.5%. This is a highly conservative investment that can yield exceptional returns, and yet you only need to deal with it once a year.

Or, say that your available funds were limited, you could have bought just 50 shares of each stock and invested just half as much, or $6,264. You would still have realized the 19% on your investment, but your commissions would have been slightly higher due to the odd lot order of less than 100 shares.

Typical commissions with a discount broker would be in the 1% to 2% range, which reduces your yearly gain by a similar amount. If you would like more information on the O'Higgins Dow-beating System, his book and newsletter are available:

Beating The Dow, by Michael O'Higgins, 1991, Harper Collins Publishers ($19.95)

Newsletter: Beating the Dow, The Hirsch Organization, Inc., 184 Central Avenue, Trail, Old Tappan, NJ 07675 (12 issues $125.00). Telephone number (201) 767-4100.

Key Point: This system is undoubtedly the simplest and least expensive way to own individual stocks and still utilize a money manager who has been in the top 1% of all money managers for the past three years. Most such money managers require a $50,000 to $100,000 minimum investment and charge an annual fee of typically 1.5% to 3.0% of the amount managed.

By managing the portfolio yourself and by using the Beating the Dow by Higgins, you avoid minimum and management fees altogether. Beating the Dow with this system is a low risk, low cost, high return vehicle that is ideal for utilizing the wealth building potential of long term compounding. This is especially true if the investment is funded and maintained in any of the tax deferred plans such as an IRA or other retirement plan.

Also, it becomes readily apparent that the higher the annual rate of compounding is, the faster your investment will grow and the greater your accumulation of wealth will be. This allows some investors to reach their goal earlier or to retire at an earlier date.

PART III: Income Property — Apartments

Chapter 6: The Rental Apartment Advantage

One of the most compelling reasons for owning real estate is its proven ability to grow in value faster than the rate of inflation. This, coupled with real estate's unique ability to shelter substantial income from taxes, largely explains why the wealthy hold a major share of their wealth in real estate — second only to their holdings in the stock market. Although these are also important reasons for the beginning investor as well — even more important is the opportunity to employ very high leverage debt. Leverage which can help the beginning investor multiply a small down payment into huge profits.

When I speak of real estate, I must admit to a strong bias for apartment rentals. But let's look at the other possibilities for comparison purposes. If a person buys land it's with the expectation that it can be held for a period of time and then sold at a profit. Even if a person makes the right decision about the land and it does appreciate in price, and it's eventually sold at a profit, there is an overwhelming downside, especially for the small investor. This is that the land will not generate any income to fund the installment payments that must be made when property is purchased with a small down payment. Another important disadvantage is that one must pay property taxes every year on a property that produces no income, a dead loss, even if one owns the property free and clear of debt. On the other hand, apartment rental property purchased at an advantageous price and then improved, will not only make your mortgage payments, and other expenses, including property taxes, but will provide you with at least a small income. An income that will grow as you make improvements to your property and raise rents. And when you sell your property at a handsome profit, a substantial capital gain will be realized if you bought and managed your property well.

I will now compare commercial rental property such as office, retail or industrial. One of the biggest disadvantages, particularly for a small investor, is that you may only have one or two tenants. If one tenant moves out, you have a 50% vacancy factor and if the other one moves, you have 100%. This can result in a devastating loss to you as weeks or even months go by while you attempt to find a suitable tenant. This must be a tenant who finds your space suitable to his particular business, and that zoning laws in your area will permit him to occupy. Contrast this with one or two tenants moving out of an eight unit apartment building, with the resulting vacancy factor of only 12% to 25%. And then, more often than not, you are only going to lose a few days of rent, if any, as a well located, well maintained, and reasonably priced unit will draw a strong response of prospective renters. If you have required your renters to give 30 days notice of moving — or they forfeit their deposit, you will have ample time in which to re-rent the unit without any loss.

It's been my experience that ownership of rental units offers the greatest potential return, with the lowest risk of any real estate investment. This is true, however, only if purchased at a favorable price. Since price, and also terms, are pivotal in buying a property that will become a successful investment, I will describe what considerations need to be made, and then the process itself of buying income property.
My concept, which is similar to what many successful real estate investors follow, is rather simple and highly profitable. It has allowed me to purchase ten different properties with anywhere from two to 41 units each, in three different states. These all have been purchased with small down payments and favorable terms. The concept is essentially this: buy property that needs improvement at a below-market price — 10% or more — and low down payment —10% or less — make the improvements, raise the rents, and sell or trade the property for a profit. You can do this, or

hold the property for appreciation and tax sheltered income.

Of course improvements cost money, so we are only interested in "light fixers." These include improvements such as inside or outside paint, minor repairs, clean-up or minor re-landscape, carpet or vinyl replacement in a limited number of rooms. Any improvement that doesn't cost thousands, that is recoverable in increased rents, or for which you have the funds, should be considered. A few of the improvements that may not cost you anything, and that might actually save you money are: replacement of a poor on-site manager, or contracting for coin laundry machines at no cost to you and a 50% share of proceeds taken in. One could also put common area lights on timers to reduce electric bills, or change subcontractors such as trash pick-up, snow removal or pest control at reduced rates or less frequent service. These are just a few of many possibilities that may reduce your costs without taking away anything from your tenants.

Now it might seem we've gotten away from the concept a bit with these cost saving ideas. However, keep in mind that any improvement that is made is with the thought that it will improve the bottom line profits. By reducing costs, one causes the property to show increased spendable income, which is worth a higher price when sold. If the units are retained, greater spendable income on into the future is available. In any event, now that the concept has been identified, we need to identify what constitutes buying the property at a favorable price and terms and exactly what buying procedure to use in order to insure the purchase of property that will be highly profitable to you This and the specific steps to take in buying a property will be covered in the following chapters.

Key Points: Ownership of rental income units is the least risky choice for owning investment-type property. The other advantages are the wealth building natures of such an investment including use of leverage, appreciation in value and capital gains, and tax sheltered growth and income. The concept in its simplest form involves buying low, improving the property and its cash flow, and selling high, or at least selling at the higher price that your improvements and increased cash flow will allow. My rental properties were all purchased using this concept and all have been highly successful investments.

Chapter 7: How To Get Started

Another big advantage of owning your own rental property is that you control the investment completely. Contrast that with owning property through a limited partnership investment, where the general partner makes all the decisions and takes his fees right off the top and continues to draw management fees regularly. Direct ownership of the property allows you to realize all the profits of the investment, including the option to manage and improve the property through your own efforts therefore increasing your profits proportionately. Getting started is not as difficult as you might imagine and once you realize how tremendously profitable such an investment is over a period of time, you will feel well rewarded for the amount of time you invest.

My own first experience with rental units may be helpful in understanding this opportunity. There was an ad in the local newspaper, stating the owner of six units was only asking $32,000 with a small down payment. This was back in 1975, and just the type of property that my wife and I had been looking for and thought we could handle. What I found was four one bedroom units about 20 years old and in generally good repair, and on an adjoining parcel — a duplex about 40 years old and in need of painting and many minor repairs. The owner, retired and in his sixties, had been making repairs over several years after buying the run down property at a bargain price. Since he had made the repairs himself and there was no real estate commission to be paid, he was able to sell the property at a below market price and still make a profit. He and his wife were motivated to sell as they were tired of fixing up the property and wanted to travel. Based on other ads that we had previously checked on, this property was definitely a bargain.

Unfortunately, the small down payment asked for was $5,000, about $2,000 more than we had set aside to invest. Since the owner had several other prospective buyers, I decided to offer him full price and explain our problem with the down payment. I told him how much we liked the property, but that we were about $2,000 short of making the full down payment. I asked if he would consider taking the balance in installments. After determining that I had a good income from my own business and considering that we were young and enthusiastic first time buyers, willing to pay him full price, the owner agreed to carry back a note that would allow us to make installment payments over a six-month period. This, of course, was in addition to the payments to be made on the existing mortgage we were assuming.

After purchasing the property, we continued to make repairs. Minor repairs such as painting and landscaping we did ourselves. Other repairs involving carpentry, plumbing and electrical, we hired others to do. Over the next two years we made these improvements in our spare time and raised rents modestly as each unit was completed. At this point we felt that we had learned enough and accomplished enough to be able to sell at a profit. Our longer term goal was to be able to take the proceeds from this investment and invest in a larger property where we could afford an on-site manager.

We listed the property with a realtor who advised us to sell the four unit property and the two unit property separately, believing that our profit and his commission, would be greater. It turned out to be good advice. Within 90 days we had sold both properties, the fourplex for $30,000 and the duplex for $19,500. Here was the picture of our investment after the sale:

Total proceeds from sale before commission & fees	$49,500
Less commission, title and escrow fees	<u>- 3,375</u>
Net proceeds	46,125
Less original purchase price and escrow fees	<u>32,485</u>
Balance	13,640
Less out of pocket expenses to improve property	<u>-1,560</u>
Net profit from property sale	11,080
Plus surplus rent receipts after payment of all expenses, mortgage and property tax payments:	
year 1	2,300
year 2	<u>4,630</u>
Total return over 2 year period on $5,000 invested	18,010

Although these figures obviously reflect real estate values over twenty years past, they are still highly significant in terms of percentage return on investment. Few investments can boast over a 100% annual return as was the case here over a two year period. This investment clearly illustrates the leverage factor available in real estate that makes such returns possible. The leverage can be illustrated in this way. Assuming the investment had been for $32,000, all cash instead of $5,000 down, and the dollar return had been the same, the percentage return on an annual basis would have been only 28%.

Holding property for the long haul, rather than selling a property early on as was done here, may offer even greater advantages. This is particularly true of a property such as this that has a positive cash flow. By positive cash flow I mean that after all expenses of the property of every kind are paid, including mortgage payments and property taxes, there is cash left over for the owner. Let's examine this property to see what additional benefits we might realize if the property were held as an investment for twenty-five years, the period it would take for the mortgage to fully amortize and the property to become free and clear of debt. The projected results of holding these six units for a period of 25 years can be summarized as follows:

SUMMARY OF 6 UNITS — HELD FOR 25 YEARS

Value (purchase price) at time of purchase $32,000

Value at end of 2 years   49,000

Value at end of 25 years, assuming historical average

of 5% annual inflation /appreciation * $155,925

Less balance of mortgage owed after 25 years   -0-

Positive cash flow based on $4,600 receipts annually

for 25 yrs., reinvested at typical 6% interest **   <u>252,374</u>

     Subtotal   408,299

Less initial out-of-pocket down payment   5,000

Less initial out-of pocket improvements   1,560

Less a 6% commission on sale of 6 units   9,356

Less est. title, escrow, closing fees 2%   <u>3,119</u>

     Subtotal   19,035

     <u>-19,035</u>

Net Gain over 25 year period   389,264

* This 5% projection has proven to be realistic as the ending value of $155,925 represents approximately $26,000 per unit, which is representative of present values of similar one bedroom units.

**I've assumed that annual increases in rents would simply offset expense increases due to inflation. In my experience, since the owner controls both to some extent, rents can often be increased faster than expenses, provided the property is continually well maintained and managed.

As a buy, improve and hold strategy, this property would have produced an outstanding annual compounded return of 19% over the 25-year holding period.

<u>Key Points</u>: Buying rental properties can be extremely profitable, whether held short term or long term. The opportunity to use greater leverage safely is more readily available than in nearly any other type investment.

Rental property can often be purchased for as little as 5% to 10% down, allowing leverage of 90% to 95%. Holding property long term is especially attractive for a number of reasons: equity is built up in the property as the mortgage is paid down with rent receipts. As the property is improved from rental receipts and raised rents, the equity is further increased as the property becomes more valuable. All the while the property acts as an inflation hedge, generally increasing in over all value at about the same rate as the annual rate of inflation.

Furthermore, until the property is sold, it will be a tax shelter for all of these gains except for equity buildup resulting from mortgage pay down plus the amount of net spendable income you realize annually. Even a large part of this will be offset by the amount of depreciation — paper loss rather than actual loss — that you are allowed to deduct by tax law.

In short it is the tremendous power of compounding value and equity that is at work in such an investment that makes owning apartment rental property one of the most desirable of all wealth building alternatives.

Chapter 8: Buying Strategy

Despite the impressive wealth building possibilities of owning your own rental property, a certain strategy must be followed. Without it., one could wind up with a property that is a liability rather than a desirable asset. This strategy can best be illustrated by a property profile that will incorporate all the important factors that must be present in order for your investment to be successful:

Purchase Price: Under the market by at least 10% to 15%. This gives you a margin of error. Pricing property is not an exact science. If you buy under the market price by 15%, you automatically build into the transaction a potential profit of 15% from the start of your ownership.

Terms: The lowest down payment you can negotiate, ideally 5% to 10%, but certainly no more than 15%. The down payment can be 15% only if there are several favorable offsetting factors. Other favorable terms that we always seek are these: The existing loan is assumable by you, thereby saving you or the seller the costs and the uncertainty of new loan terms — the existing loan interest rate is below or at current market rates. Or, the property is free of debt, and the seller is willing to carry back a note payable to him or her and secured by the property— again, at or below the market interest rate. Or, new financing can be obtained and will be obtained before escrow closes, and will be subject to your approval as well as the lender's, including length of loan, interest rate, who is to pay the costs of obtaining such a loan, variable or fixed interest rate, and any balloon payment or other special terms or conditions of the loan.

Building: The age of the building that you should be interested in will typically be 10 to 30 years of age and in need of minor repairs. Such buildings are known as "light fixers." Buildings with severe roof problems, severe structural, foundation, or severe drainage or wall leak problems should be avoided. The reason is that the high cost of such repairs, and the difficulty of determining what repairs would be successful, decreases your chances of owning a rental property that can be profitably operated and eventually sold for a worthwhile profit by you.

Units: In general, you want to buy the greatest number of rental units that you have time to manage. One, two, or three bedroom units are most desirable as they bring the highest rents and are the easiest to rent in most areas. Unfurnished are preferable to furnished units because furnished units cost more to maintain and turnover more often. Studio apartments should also be avoided because of the higher rate of turnover of renters.

One of the major difficulties in buying a property at a below market value/price, is determining what the true market price is. This can most readily be determined by asking one or more of your realtors for "comparables." Comparables are what similar units, in similar condition, with similar rental income and expenses have actually sold for. A realtor dealing in rental units should be able to provide you with a list of such properties sold over the past few years. A less reliable indication of market price is a comparison of a number of current listings of similar properties currently for sale. Keep in mind that a number of these properties will be way over priced, and that nearly all will be overpriced by at least 10% to 15% just to allow room for negotiation and to cover the realtor's fee of 5% to 6%. Occasionally a property will be underpriced, in which case you will need to move quickly.

Another method of determining value is to base it on the cost approach. This method is often used by appraisers, but should only be used by you as a guideline. Never make a buying decision solely on the cost approach (Jaffe 156-175). Say we have four one-bedroom units with a total square footage of 2,600 feet. And assume that the cost per square foot to build these units new today would be $60 per foot. The value would be 2600 times $60, or $156,000. Since these units are 25 years old and are expected to have a total life of about 50 years, they reduce the value by 50% to $78,000. The land also has value and doesn't depreciate, so the current market value of such land must be added, say $30,000. This method would estimate the present value, using the cost approach, as the sum of these two figures, or a total of $108,000. Therefore total replacement value to duplicate this property new would be $186,000.

Another method used by appraisers, and the one of greatest interest to us, is the income approach. Using the same four units, and assuming they are rented for $340 per unit, the total income would be $16,320. Then the appraiser might assume a typical vacancy factor of 5%, and reduce the income by $816 for an effective gross annual income of $15,504. Then the appraiser would estimate the expenses of the property including utilities, repairs, advertising, management, insurance and property taxes — all expenses of every kind, but not mortgage and interest payments.

In this example, the expenses totaled $7,200, so the $15,504 reduced by $7,200 would give us a net operating income of $8,304.

Appraisers using the above income method, then apply a capitalization rate that calculates value based on the net operating income. This is a way of determining value that the banks often require as part of their loan application packages. This undoubtedly is the most complex method of determining value and of the least interest to us in evaluating properties. However, a basic understanding of this method does give us another tool for purposes of comparing value, arrived at by using the various methods.

Here's how it works. The appraiser evaluates several comparable sales and assigns a capitalization rate to this evaluation. This rate might typically be determined to be anything from a 7 to a 12. The rate is intended to reflect the interest return on the investment and the rate of return of the capital investment. The lower the number, the more valuable the property. In this case, an above average neighborhood of generally well maintained homes/ apartments, might justify a 9. In the preceding case, where we had a net income of $8,304, the appraiser would divide this by the cap rate of .09, to give us a value by the income approach of $92,266.

Obviously a buyer in this situation would rather buy with the price based on the income approach since it will justify a lower price than the cost approach will. On the other hand, as the new owners, to the extent that we can reduce expenses or increase rental income, we can cause the property to be appraised at a higher value. This could help to increase the selling price and profit at the time of sale.

Another tool used to determine value is one used primarily by real estate brokers based on the amount of the gross annual rent receipts of a property. Using the fourplex's gross of $16,320 as an example, if it was listed for six times gross, it would be listed for $97,920. This is a very rough rule of thumb that should never be used as the basis of determining what a property is worth, or how much should be offered on it. Despite this, it can be helpful in screening property. You certainly don't want to pay eight or ten times gross for 20 year old property when that's what new property can be bought for. Or, conversely, you might be interested in checking out the four units in the example if they were listed at only five times gross.

The method, and how one uses it determines what price one should pay for a property. The method

I use is a hybrid based on cash flow, so I will refer to it as the cash flow analysis method. Again, using the fourplex numbers as an example, we would need to know the present level of gross income ($16,320), the present expenses ($7,200) and the amount of the mortgage payment including principal and interest. To get the amount of mortgage payment, let's assume that we are considering paying up to $85,000 for the property with 10% down, $8,500, and we plan to assume the existing mortgage which is at 8% and has a balance owing of $60,000 with monthly payments of $500. The other $16,500 we are proposing the seller carry back as a second mortgage at 8% payable over a 12-year period at $178 per month, principal and interest. We subtract from the gross income of $16,320 the expenses of $7,200, and the annual payments on the first mortgage and second mortgage totaling $8,136, leaving us a potential net spendable of $984 annually (6% of gross).

This cash flow analysis would indicate to me a marginally acceptable property, possibly worth buying, depending on two other factors. One, the typical vacancy factor — which is often estimated at 5%. If this property was at that level, it would leave a spendable income of only 1% — even more marginal. However, if it was discovered that the expenses included a $60 a month allowance to one of the tenants to mow the lawn and act as part time manager, an expense that could be eliminated by doing this work ourselves, another $720 could be added to the spendable income. Secondly, suppose that the $340 a month was low for similar one-bedroom units, and that by painting the units inside and shampooing carpets, they could be rented for $365 to $385. At an average rent of $375, the spendable income could be raised by another $1,680. Now with a projected spendable income of an additional $2,400, the annual net income could be increased from $984 to $3,384 (increasing the 6% return on gross to 20%. Keep in mind that with the $8,500 (10%) down and a projected net income of $3,384 annually, we would be realizing a 39% annual return on the cash invested. Based on this cash flow analysis, I would judge this property worth pursuing at the target price of $85,000 or less.

Based on the cash flow analysis method, properties should be rejected that cannot be purchased for a price that will allow a net spendable of 5% to 10% or more. Properties with marginal net spendable can be considered if two conditions exist. One, certain expenses can obviously be reduced, and two, rents can be increased quickly with minor cosmetic improvements.

As you begin to look for your first property, be patient. Many properties won't even come close to meeting the prescribed requirements. Don't hesitate to ask for actual income and actual expense statements on any property you may be interested in. Also, don't be taken in by broker projections on properties that are promoted based on their potential income. Insist on paying no more than what a property is worth now, based on actual figures and your own cash flow analysis. Compare reported income and expenses for the property under consideration with the income and expenses of other properties. This will help you to verify the accuracy of the prospective property reports and help familiarize you with rent levels and typical expenses of a variety of other properties. When it comes time to make an offer, make the offer contingent on your inspection and verification of all items of expenses and all rental agreements, including rents and deposits.

As you begin the process of looking for your first property, don't be disappointed if you can't find a property in the first few weeks that is suitable in terms of a successful profile. Finding a property with the right profile and one that can also meet the requirements of cash flow analysis can take many months. The national economy and particularly the local economy and housing and apartment availability largely determines how difficult it is to find a suitable property. In periods of prosperity, demand for rental units is high, rents are increasing and most properties are fully priced, and many overpriced. During periods of recession, rents are soft and declining, prices of property are generally in decline and the least desirable and most expensive apartments are increasingly difficult to rent. Ideally, as such a period ends, as witnessed by gradually increasing rents and an improving local economy, this represents the best opportunity to safely buy rental units. During such periods of recession, the building of new apartments nearly stops and the improvement of existing apartments slows down as rents decline and the cash flow available to owners tightens up. As the economy improves and employment and wages improve,, the demand for well maintained apartments increases — right at the time that the availability of such units is at its lowest. If you buy during such a period, you can improve your apartments, raise rents and the income and value of your apartments will increase. As the economy improves, you can continue to raise rents and subsequently the value of your apartments as well.

The mid 1990s appears to be just such an ideal buying period. However, given other periods when normal economic conditions prevail, why would some owners be willing to sell to you below market or below the appraised value, and often on favorable terms as well? As you have already learned, there can be major differences in value depending on what method of determining value or price is used. Differences of 5% to 10% are common and sometimes the difference, can be as much as 15% to 20%. Given this range, sellers are often more flexible in price than one might expect. This is just one of many reasons that owners will sell well below what a property may be worth. Knowing the many other reasons to look for can give you a bargaining edge:

[1] Illness or death of the owner, requiring disposition of the property quickly.

[2] Property has been "milked." A shortsighted owner has quit making repairs or otherwise not maintained the property and, as he "milks" off the extra profit and the vacancy rate increases, he eventually has to sell rather than dig into his own funds to make the apartments rentable again.

[3] Owner loses his regular job and needs to sell the property in order to get his equity out to live on.

[4] Owner is transferred to another city or state and does not wish to pay a management company to manage the property,

[5] Owner is retiring from his regular job and/ or desires to retire from the part time demands of apartment ownership.

[6] Fear of negative local or national economic conditions, particularly if there is pressure to lower rents and the vacancy factor is increasing.

[7] Family matters such as divorce, moving away to be near children or grandchildren, or just the desire to travel or be away without the responsibilities of apartment ownership.

[8] Disenchantment with the apartment rental business. Owners may have paid too much for the apartments and are disappointed with the return on their investment. They may have mismanaged the apartments and instead of realizing a spendable return, are digging into other funds in order to pay the bills. This is known as "feeding" the apartments, and when this happens, this will be one of your most motivated seller — sometimes willing to practically give the property away and on very favorable (to you) terms.

Whatever the reason, the longer the property is on the market and not sold, the better your chances are of buying the property below market value and on terms favorable to you. All of these considerations fit together. A property that fits the profile and passes the cash flow analysis can usually be acquired for a below market price and on favorable terms. This will be illustrated in the next chapter as we review and analyze an actual purchase made in the late 1980s.

Key Points: Buying rental apartment property involves a certain strategy that must be followed in order to be successful. The key to this strategy is buying at least 10% below market price with a low down payment of 5% to 10% and low interest rate. The building itself should be 10 to 30 years old and in need of light fixing.

Determining the true market price/value can most readily be accomplished by studying "comparable" sales of similar properties in recent years. However, it is also important to know how appraisers value property based on the "cost" method, the "income" method, or the "times gross" method.

The most meaningful method of determining what you should pay for a property is the "cash flow analysis method." This method requires that you only consider property that will generate at least 5% to 10% of positive cash flow (net spendable). For this reason, in dealing with brokers, you must insist that income and the value of the property must be based on what the property is actually doing, not the broker's projection of what the property should be doing or is capable of doing in the future.

Because the property should fit the recommended profile, you must be prepared to be patient until such a property is found.

There are many reasons why sellers will often sell their properties well below what the property is worth and well below their asking price. Delving for the reasons which range from poor economic conditions to many types of personal problems or special circumstances can provide a bargaining edge. In any event, the longer the property is on the market and remains unsold, the greater are your chances of buying below market and on the most favorable terms.

Chapter 9: The Village Apartments, A Case History

Back in the late 1980s, my wife and I set out to look for suitable apartments in the northwest part of the country. Our objective was to find 20 to 40 units that could be managed by others, that offered strong positive cash flow, and that produced income which could be largely sheltered from taxes. During this period the national economy, and particularly the real estate market in the Northwest, was generally depressed. However, there were early signs of some improvement. Unemployment was beginning to go down and there were some notes of optimism — of improving business and interest rates trending down.

As we began our search, we noticed that most of the apartments listed in the area newspaper were only two to eight units and only after talking to a couple of real estate brokers did we finally find twelve two-bedroom units to consider. They had just been listed. The property was only about five or six years old, well maintained, in a good neighborhood, and they were asking $385,000 with a down payment of $50,000. Income per unit averaged $325 per month, or about $47,000 per year, and their expenses were fairly low as this was a nearly new building. Quickly dividing the asking price by the income, we came up with over 8 times gross, which told me the property was probably too expensive for our purposes, but probably near market price. Dividing the asking price by the number of units, we came up with $32,000 per unit; backing out $2,000 per unit for the land, we came up with a replacement cost of about $30,000 per unit. Since we estimated a new unit could be built for about $25,000 to $30,000 each, we decided this property was probably overpriced and decided not to investigate it any further.

About two weeks later an ad appeared in the newspaper for 20 units for $495,000 with only 10% down. This appeared promising, so we decided to drive by the property. The units, all one-bedroom, were located in two two-story buildings; all the lower units had private, fenced in patios, and the upper units had patio decks with wood perimeter and handrails. Ordinarily this would be a nice feature, but in this case we noticed that most of the upper deck hand rails were badly warped and some of the vertical pieces were missing or broken. Even worse, we noticed that parts of the patio fencing had collapsed and in the patios and yard areas were discarded furniture, appliances, toys and, most disturbing, bits and pieces of asphalt shingles (from the roof). Examining the roof, even from a distance, it appeared that it had suffered considerable wind damage. Examining the building further, it appeared that it had recently been painted, but many of the screen/storm doors were in need of repairs, or screen or glass replacement. In general, it appeared that this 12 to 14 year old building had been "milked." Once the rent they were able to get declined enough to hurt, and the vacancy factor pinched income even more, they decided to sell.

Apparently the previous year there had been a severe windstorm causing damage to the roofs which they probably found would cost far more to repair than they were willing to spend — further motivating them to sell. However, it appeared that they had decided to paint the buildings as the least expensive way to make them more saleable. Nonetheless, we decided to review the figures on the property to see if this "not so light fixer" would be worth pursuing further. With an annual income of $66,000 ($275 per unit), the asking price of $395,000 figured out to be 7.5 times gross. Too much for a building in obvious need of extensive exterior (and probably interior) repairs and what would likely be a roof repair/replacement running into the thousands. As a double check, an assumed replacement cost of $395,000 divided by 20 units, worked out to $19,750 less a couple thousand per unit for land, or $17,750. The question was, could you build a similar one bedroom unit for this amount? And the answer was no, but you could probably build such units for $20,000 to $23,000.

Then the question was, for a discount of $2,000 to $5,000 per unit, or $40,000 to $100,000 overall, would you rather have these units, or brand new units? Given the extensive repairs needed, and the additional cash required to make such repairs over and above the $50,000 cash down payment, this property didn't fit our profile. Primarily because it was not a light fixer and secondarily, it did not appear that we could buy it well below the market or even well below replacement cost once deferred maintenance and depreciation were factored in. Therefore, we continued to look.

After several disappointments, about a month and a half later we saw an ad in the paper that really looked promising, but possibly out of our range. Our objective had been to put no more than $50,000 down and to keep a reserve of $15,000 to $20,000 to make improvements as needed and as a margin of safety. This property was 40 units and they were only asking $700,000, but they wanted $100,000 down. The property was located in a town of about 20,000 people, about 16 miles out from a major city. We drove by the property ourselves and were immediately impressed with the neighborhood, but more than a little disappointed in the outward appearance of the apartments.

The neighborhood was attractive, mostly middle income single family homes, with one smaller apartment of eight units and a larger and newer property of about 60 apartment units. Within a block was a hospital and park, and public transportation and shopping were only two to three blocks away. The Village Apartments were obviously the ugly duckling of the neighborhood. They were painted a sort of mustard color, the parking lot was scarred with chuck holes and in need of seal coating, and trees and bushes were overgrown everywhere. On the positive side, we noticed that the roofing on all six buildings was new, that each unit had a new storm/screen door, and the buildings appeared well designed and well built. In any event, we viewed the problems we saw as cosmetic and not terribly expensive to correct. The major questions now were the interior condition of the units and how flexible the seller was on price and terms.

In talking to the broker, we learned that the seller was very motivated and willing to consider any reasonable offer. The property had been "milked" which explained the run-down condition. The owner, quite elderly, had hired an on-site manager who was making some progress in raising rents and reducing the vacancy factor. Nonetheless, the owner didn't want to put enough money into the property to make it into a better moneymaker. He was more interested in getting his equity out and getting on with his retirement.

Since taking over, the owners had accumulated only nine months of receipt and expenditure records to offer us. By projecting these for another three months, we came up with the following picture: Income $108,000, $225 per unit average, all expenses except mortgage payments, $53,000, and net $55,000 before mortgage payments. On a times gross basis, if we offered $650,000, we would be paying six times gross which seemed reasonable for this property.

The key question then was, would it pass the cash flow analysis test? We found that we could assume a first mortgage of $487,000 with interest at 9.75% and payments of $5,626 or $67,512 per year. Obviously, with net income of only $55,000 and mortgage payments of $67,512, we would have negative cash flow of over $12,000 per year plus the annual payment on a second mortgage of $63,000, even if we came up with $100,000 down. Obviously this wouldn't work out for us cash flow wise, and we didn't want to put $100,000 down.

We expressed this to the broker and he indicated that there might be a solution to this problem. The seller would just as soon refinance the property and get more cash out anyway. Assuming that we could buy the property for $650,000 with 10% down and finance the balance of $585,000 for 25 years, we could get the total mortgage payment down to $58,800/ yearly or $4,900 monthly — only $3,000 from breaking even. This looked better but we still wanted to create positive cash flow after all expenses, even though part of that mortgage payment would be income to us in the form of paying down the mortgage balance and therefore increasing our equity in the property.

Finally, as we analyzed the rental records of the property, we came up with an answer. We noticed that individual units were rented for anywhere from $210 per unit to $275 per unit, and that the last ten units rented were at $245. From looking at other properties, we noticed that two bedroom units typically rented for $250 to $300. We reran the numbers and at $245 per unit, gross income would increase to $117,600, which would wipe out the $3,000 negative cash flow and give us $6,600 positive cash flow or spendable. Assuming that we made additional improvements over the following year and raised the average up to $275, we would increase our annual cash flow by an additional $14,400 (to $132,000 annually), bringing our total positive cash flow to $21,000. With a potential near term positive cash flow of 16% of gross, the Village Apartments were beginning to look very interesting.

We still had the problem of 10% down or $65,000 which was $15,000 more than what we were prepared to put down. Here again, the broker — wanting to make a sale — had a suggestion. He felt that most, if not all, of this difference could be made up in escrow as we would be credited the amount of rent deposits held ($150 x 40 units = $6,000) and the pro-rated rent, (one month's rent collected in advance, $225 x 40 units = $9,000), would also be credited to us as new owners.

Since renters must pay their rent 30 days in advance, assuming all rents have been paid before the first of the month when escrow closes, then all advance rents are due (credited) the buyer. In the same sense, since rent deposits paid in advance must eventually be refunded to the renters, the new owner/ buyer should be credited with the total amount of deposits held by the seller.

Based on the information we had, we decided to make an offer of $600,000 with $60,000 down, contingent on refinancing the property on terms acceptable to us and crediting us in escrow for rental deposits and prepaid rent. Further contingencies included our inspection of all units to determine if their condition was acceptable to us, and that all appliances, equipment and plumbing would be in good working order. The seller was agreeable to our contingencies but countered that $650,000 was the least they would accept and that they wanted $75,000 down. We told the broker that the counter offer was acceptable to us except for the amount of the down. We suggested that if the broker would contribute $19,500 cash of his commission (about $32,500) toward the down, we would be willing to repay him with a note for the same amount due in one year. Because this was a sale on a property he had been trying to sell for more than a year, he quickly agreed. (We expected to repay him mostly from the positive cash flow of the property).

Next came our inspection of the property. As we looked at the exterior and the interior of every unit, we made extensive notes on the condition of carpet, paint, appliances, tile, plumbing and what equipment and maintenance equipment was present and in what condition. Our purpose was as follows:

To estimate what costs of repair or cosmetic improvement we might face in order to bring rental rates up to $245 or $275. We later estimated these costs to be $15,000 - $20,000. We also determined what costs we might be able to cause the seller to incur prior to our takeover which would reduce the amount of expense for us later. On this point we found a kitchen and a bath sink with serious leaks, a stove and refrigerator needing repair and the central swimming pool filter and motor needing repair. In addition, we found a new snow blower and weed whip along with various tools for maintenance and cleaning which we determined we would require to be left in order to save us that expense. In all, we felt about $2,500 to $3,000 could be saved by making all of these a requirement of our contingency, which we did.

Because the lender selected by the seller was unwilling to make the loan at this time, the seller reluctantly agreed to carry back $100,000 as a second mortgage payable at $719 per month. This included 8.75% interest only, $50,000 due in three years and the other $50,000 in six years. This was acceptable to us as we felt we could get a new loan in the first three years before the first note would be due. Based on all points now being agreed to by buyer and seller, escrow was now closed. **[See Figure 8]**

FIGURE 8

PIONEER TITLE COMPANY
OF CANYON COUNTY

NAMPA, IDAHO

TITLE INSURANCE · ESCROWS

CLOSING STATEMENT

LLER: K, DAVID A. & WANDA I.   ADDRESS: ID

YER: KEITHLEY FAMILEY TRUST   PRORATION DATE: October 6, 1989

OKER: ALL AMERICAN REALTY   LOAN NO.

CROW OFFICER: DESIREE A. MAYDEN   ESCROW NO. PN17024

	Debit	Credit
LES PRICE: $650,000.00	650,000.00	
RNEST MONEY PD. TO: ALL AMERICAN REALTY (less appraisal)		12,550.00
POSIT INTO ESCROW		
AN AMOUNT IN FAVOR OF SELLER – All Inclusive Deed of Trust		487,500.00
AN AMOUNT IN FAVOR OF SELLER – All Inclusive Deed of Trust		100,000.00
TEREST @		
SERVES: Taxes Mo. @		
Fire Ins. Mo. @		
FHA MI Mo. @		
AN ORIGINATION FEE		
AN DISCOUNT FEE %		
EDIT REPORT		
PRAISAL FEE SELLER TO REIMBURSE BUYER ½ of $2,450.00		1,225.00
AN PAYOFF		
AN ASSUMED:		
NTEREST		
ESERVES		
TRACT OF SALE:		
ROW FILING FEE: WEST ONE BANK, Each ½ of $85.00 (COLLECTION LEDGER)	42.50	
AN ASSUMPTION FEE:		
TER: NO SEARCH MADE		
IGATION: NAMPA MERIDIAN 1989 $50.26 Seller 1-1 to 10-6; Buyer 10-6 o 12-31; 1988 – SELLER AMOUNTS	11.34	
D. NONE SHOWN OF RECORD		
ES: PAID THROUGH UNDERLYING LOAN; Buyer to credit seller /31 of October taxes at closing; additionally monthly outside closing	838.71	
E INSURANCE STATE FARM, Buyer cost outside closing 2nd ½; 1st ½ to be paid through closing	1,123.80	
LE INSURANCE PIONEER TITLE COMPANY, Seller cost		
ORDING WARRANTY DEED, DEEDS OF TRUSTS, UCC-1, Each ½ of	17.50	
TORNEY FEE EACH PARTY TO PAY RESPECTIVE FEES OUTSIDE CLOSING		
OKER'S COMMISSION ALL AMERICAN REALTY, Seller cost		
OAN AMOUNT IN FAVOR OF ALL AMERICAN REALTY, Buyer credit		19,500.00
OKERS COMMISSION – WESTMARK REAL ESTATE, Seller cost		
T PRORATIONS (provided by seller), credit to buyer		4,336.13
URITY DEPOSITS, credit to buyer (provided by seller)		4,790.00
ROW WITHHOLD:		
ROW CLOSING FEE: PIONEER TITLE COMPANY, Buyer cost		300.00
ANCE DUE THIS ESCROW AN BUYERS COST		22,430.67
TAL	652,343.85	652,343.85

[handwritten annotations: "My initial deposit out-of-pocket", "My pro-rated share of rents", "security deposits refunded to me", "My other out-of-pocket expenses @ close of escrow"]

We hereby certify that the foregoing is a true and correct statement of funds received and disbursed by us in the above closing.

We, the undersigned, have read and approved the above closing statement.
KEITHLEY FAMILY TRUST

BY: _____

BY: _____

PIONEER TITLE COMPANY OF CANYON COUNTY

BY: _____
    DESIREE A. MAYDEN

Date: _____ October 11, 1989

As you can see in Figure 8, the closing statement, my only out-of-pocket down payment and expense was the $12,500 earnest money plus $22,430 shown due as balance of buyer's cost — in total $34,930, or just 5% of the purchase price. Obviously the $19,500 realtors commission carried back as a note by the realty instead of taking cash, and the $4,338 and $4,790 prorations of rent and deposits, made this possible. I go into this amount of detail to illustrate how it is possible to buy property with a low down payment.

Now that we owned the property, we instituted several expense reducing ideas (more about that in the next chapter on management), began making repairs and cosmetic improvements and, as units became vacant, improved them and raised rents. Also after about three months of making such improvements, inside and out, we raised all rents on existing tenants to the $275 level except for about six or eight units where the tenants had been there for four or five years or longer. After the first full year of operation our income and expense looked like this:

Village Apartments

Incomes (rents, retained deposits and laundry)	**$133,518**
Expenses:	
Utilities	**$11,334**
Maintenance	**$18,928**
Manager	**$7,400**
Advertising & office	**$1,355**
Miscellaneous expense	**$ 812**
Insurance	**$2,529**
Property tax	**$12,078**
Interest 1st & 2nd mortgages	**$55,549**
Security deposit refunds	**1,924**
Total	**111,909**
NET INCOME BEFORE DEPRECIATION	
& INCOME TAX	**$21,609**

As shown above, we had been able to hold our expenses in line while increasing our gross income above our projection of $132,000, and above our net or positive cash flow target of $21,000 plus equity build up of approximately $4,000. In this year and in the following two years we put an approximate average of $15,000 annually back into the property in order to make additional improvements and to continue to raise rents up to or nearer market rates.

Late in the third year we decided we were ready to refinance the property. Mortgage interest rates were down and it would give us an opportunity to pay off the existing first mortgage and the $100,000 that were coming due. The lower mortgage rates also would increase our net cash flow. The lender we selected asked that an independent appraisal of our property be made and indicated that they would lend up to 65% of that appraisal at an interest rate of 8.5% to 9%, and they required a year ending statement for the previous three years. **[See Figure 9]**

Figure 9 is the statement that we provided them for our third year of operation. Based on this true statement and verification, plus physical inspection of the property and comparison of the village rents and expenses to other rental properties in the general area and finally on what similar properties had sold for in the general area, an appraisal of $955,000 was arrived at. This meant we could pay off the existing first and second mortgages, all the loan and escrow fees, and pocket the remaining $54,000. We actually received a check from escrow of $114,224.48, though $60,000 was a reimbursement for that amount of the second mortgage paid from personal funds. That left us the $54,000 that we were able to pocket. The

FIGURE 9

VILLAGE APARTMENTS
INCOME STATEMENT - 1993
YEAR ENDING

INCOME:			
Rents	$164,642		
Misc. Income	2,798		
Total Income			$167,000
UTILITIES:			
Electric	4,130		
Water, Sewer & Trash	5,867		
Telephone	842		
Total		10,839	
MAINTENANCE:			
Supplies:	6,878		
Labor	12,854		
Total Maintenance		19,732	
ADMINISTRATIVE			
Manager Earnings	9,670		
Advertising	503		
Legal & Professional	1,756		
Security Deposit Refunds	1,640		
Total Administrative		13,569	
TAXES & INSURANCE			
Property Taxes	11,500		
Property Insurance	1,633		
Total Taxes & Insurance		13,133	
MORTGAGE INTEREST:			
Interest First Mortgage	50,619		
Interest Second & Third	8,632		
Second (pd. off $60,000)	000		
Total Interest		59,251	
Total All Expenses			116,524
NET INCOME			$ 50,916
CAPITAL EXPENDITURES:			
Mortgage Principal		6,267	
Capital Improvements:			
Pool Upgrade	2,661		
Air Cond. Units	670		
Carpets & Vinyl	3,973		
Draperies	532		
Refrig. & Stove	1,175		
Water Heaters	649		
Paint Upgrade	12,808		
Total Capital Improvements		22,468	
Total Mtg. Princ. & Improvements			28,735
CASH FLOW			22,181

remaining part of the second mortgage, $41,423.94 was paid out of the escrow. **[See Figure 8.1]** At the same time, by having one mortgage at 8.875% for 25 years, our annual net income, not including mortgage pay down — equity buildup, would continue at the $50,000 level now that we had caught up with deferred maintenance and capital improvements.

Now let's see how this investment looked after four years and then sum up the investment after 25 years. Before doing so, we will calculate how much of an investment we have made over the four years in order to determine our overall rate of return over the entire 25 years. The amount invested can be summarized as follows:

Cash out of pocket at time of purchase	**$34,930**
Note paid realtor 1 yr. after purchase	**19,500**
Average annual improvements, $15,00 per	
year in addition to maintenance x 3 =	**45,000**
Total	**99,430**
Reimbursed out of refinanced surplus finds	**-54,224**
Total net investment in Village Apartments	**$45,206**

The projected results of owning the Village Apartments for a 25 year period (Hicks 249-256):

FIGURE 8.1   TRANSAMERICA TITLE
1200 SIXTH AVENUE
SUITE 605
SEATTLE, WA 98101

ESTIMATED CLOSING STATEMENT

M.C. KEITHLEY,   CLOSING DATE 2/18/94
             and BETTY JEAN KEITHLEY,   ESCROW NUMBER 93-18-0437
Co-Trustees if the KEITHLEY FAMILY   RE: Village
TRUST,

	DEBITS	CREDITS
EICHLER, FAYNE & ASSOC. CHARGES:		
INTEREST (11 days @ $151.97)	1,671.67	
LOAN ORIGINATION	10,937.50	
REALTY TAX SERVICE FEES	72.00	
CREDIT REPORT	90.00	
FLOOD CERTIFICATE	39.00	
INSPECTION and MISC. EXPENSE	350.00	
INSURANCE RESERVE IMPOUND (6 mos.)	1,015.98	
TAX RESERVE (4 mos.)	4,097.24	
LENDER'S ATTORNEY FEES	1,500.00	
COMPLETION REPAIR	938.00	
BALANCE OF APPLICATION COSTS	1,229.55	
OTHER FEES:		
PAYOFF WEST ONE BANK 1st Mortgage	442,023.21	
PAYOFF WEST ONE BANK 2nd Mortgage	41,423.94	
TITLE INSURANCE (Lenders Policy)	2,466.75	
TITLE INSURANCE ENDORSEMENTS	50.00	
ESCROW FEE	1,087.50	
ESCROW FEE - SALES TAX	89.18	
RECORDING FEES	400.00	
FEDERAL EXPRESS	150.00	
RELEASE FEES	200.00	
STATE FARM INSURANCE	944.00	
NEW LOAN FROM EICHLER		525,000.00
DUE FROM BORROWER		114,224.48
TOTAL	510,775.52	510,775.52

[handwritten annotations: "Payoff of part of $100,000 2nd mortgage"; "This is the amount of the check received - less $60,000; left us $54,000 to pocket"]

ACCEPTED AND APPROVED AS TO CONTENT AND FORM:

BY: _____
    M.C.KEITHLY,

BY: _____
    BETTY JEAN KEITHLEY, CO-TRUSTEE OF THE
    KEITHLEY FAMILY TRUST

Village Apartments - 25 Year Summary

Purchase price	$650,000
Appraised Value after 4 years	955,000
Value at end of 21 additional years, assuming historical average of 5% annual inflation	$2,659,675
Less balance on $625,000 mortgage after 21 years	<u>-209,375</u>
NET VALUE	2,450,300
Average net spendable cash $15,000 x 4 years	60,000
Average net spendable $50,000 per year invested at 6% over 21 year period**	<u>$1,999,600</u>
TOTAL VALUE OF INVESTMENT AFTER 25 YEARS	$4,509,900
Less total initial net invested	-45,206
Less 6% commission on sale of units	-159,193
Less 2% est. for title & escrow fees	<u>-53,193</u>
LESS SUBTOTAL	277,979
NET GAIN OVER 25 YEAR PERIOD	$4,251,921

**Assumes conservatively that future rent increases will be entirely offset by future increases in property expenses. (In fact, two years later, spendable income had already increased to $60,000 as rents were increased and expenses held to a small increase.)

Key Points: To be sure that you are buying a wealth building property, a certain strategy and profile must be employed. Buying property at least 5% to 10% below market price and with a low down payment and otherwise favorable terms is the basic strategy. Based on the cash flow analysis method, you will only be interested in properties with a 5% to 10% or more net cash flow or what is often referred to as net spendable — the net left after all expenses of the property are paid, including principal and interest on the mortgage.

Buying such property is typically easier than one might expect. There are many reasons apartment properties are listed for sale and, because some are quite compelling, it is often helpful to know what the reason is. The more anxious or motivated a seller is, and the longer the property has been on the market, the more likely you will be able to make a good buy that meets — or often exceeds — your expectations.

That was the case with the Village Apartments. Through patient negotiations we were able to purchase the property for $650,000 with only 5% ($34,930) out-of-pocket.

Projecting our return on this investment over a 25 year period, we were delighted to learn that our likely rate of return over this period would be in excess of 20% compounded annually. In effect, the $650,000 apartments that we had purchased for 5% down, we expected to grow to a value of over $4,000,000 over this 25-year period. Although wealth building at this rate can be exciting, it is not unique. Other investors who are serious about their investment in rental apartments have reported similar or even greater eye-popping results.

The key to such high returns is leverage. In real estate investments, 5% to 10% down payments are common, as are returns of 15% to 20%. Contrast this with an investment in a money market account where a 100% payment is required for a 5% to 8% return, or a stock or bond investment where at least 50% payment is required. The fact that apartment rental property also produces income and equity buildup while providing some tax shelter, is the reason why such property is the investment choice of many of the wealthy, and provides one of the strongest wealth building alternatives that is available to nearly anyone.

Chapter 10: Rental Management & Investor Techniques To Expand Your Wealth

How a property is managed by the owner or manager is just as important and potentially just as profitable as the price and terms of the sale. To see how this process works, I will use the Village Apartments as an example.

Administrative

The first thing we noticed was that the written rental/ lease agreement did not provide a penalty for occupancies of less than six months, and the rental deposit of $100 was inadequate and below the amount typically required by other properties. In order to offset the expenses created by apartment vacancies, we amended the rental agreement to require occupancy of a unit for a minimum of six months, or the renter would lose his entire deposit. To make this penalty stronger, we raised the deposit to $150. Then, in order to motivate renters to leave their apartments clean and in good repair, we provided in the agreement for return of their full deposit for doing so, less $50 was to be used to shampoo carpets for the next occupant. The effect was significant. First of all, over the next several years, the deposits we held were increased by $50 per unit for approximately 25 of the newly rented units. This provided us with an additional $1250 of capital to use in the improvement of the apartments. In addition, those renters who failed to occupy their unit for at least six months — about seven per year — provided us with an additional income of $1,050 per year. Other benefits that are more difficult to quantify included reduced turnover, lower cost of cleaning and repair, reduced advertising expense, and reduced loss of rent due to vacancies.

In the second and third years we raised the rental deposit to $200 and then to $250, again increasing capital available to make improvements by another $2,000 to $2,500. Overall, just the tightening up of our month to month rental agreement and increasing the amount of deposit gave us a boost in income, a reduction in expenses, and an increase in funds held that we could utilize to make improvements.

In order to encourage payment of rent when due, within five days, we added a late payment charge of $20 and incorporated it into our rental-lease agreement. Although it had the desired result of reducing the number of late payments, it also increased our annual income by a couple hundred dollars as well.

Another potential for increased profits is the technique of examining every category of expense for possible reduction. Again, the Village Apartments offers us a good example of many of the other areas that can be addressed that will lower expenses, thus raising profits. Let's look at each area:

Insurance:

We found the fire and liability insurance (written by an old line company) was costing over $2,500 per year. By contacting three other insurance companies for competitive bids, we found we could get essentially the same coverage from State Farm for $1600.

Utilities:

We didn't think we would be able to reduce utilities by much since the individual units were metered and paid their own electricity. Our bill included only water, trash collection and common area lighting. However, we found that the local water district was willing to give us new, water saving shower heads for only a couple of dollars each. And also, by hooking our landscape watering system to their irrigation system for five months out of the year for a flat rate fee per year, we could decrease our cost of city water while obtaining a nearly limitless supply of water for landscape use during the spring and summer.

In addition we found that common area lighting was accomplished by several spot lights, an expensive method. We found that by replacing these incandescent lights with more efficient halogen lights, our electric cost could also be reduced.

Also, we found that we could save on trash collection. Simply by ordering smaller collection bins, these to be picked up more often, a substantial savings could be realized.

Overall, the utility bill the following year was reduced to $10,974, a savings of $350. Although this was not a huge savings in itself, it was enough to cover the cost of new shower heads and the one time hookup to the irrigation water. Even more important, now we were able to expand watering and beautify our landscape without incurring additional expense. Also, during this same period, it was significant that we had increased the amount of water and electricity being used in the coin laundry. This was due to the fact that we had doubled the number of washers and dryers installed and available to our tenants. Although this increased our income, it was accomplished without an increase in the overall utility bill because of the other savings that we had accomplished.

Still another area that we found to represent a savings was the offer of certain suppliers to discount their bill for payment with cash or within ten days of billing. Hardware and lumber companies were the most likely to agree to such discounts, and in our experience, discounts of 5% to 10% were often available.

Manager:

We found the manager to be adequately paid, $5,800 or about 5% to 6% of gross annual rent receipts, typical for management of a complex this size. In addition, she was provided an apartment and utilities paid by owners. Also, for any non-management duties beyond 20 hours per month such as cleaning and repairs, they were paid additional compensation at an hourly rate.

Although this arrangement appeared equitable, we added an incentive financial bonus to provide additional compensation for accomplishing goals that would increase our bottom line profits. These goals involved filling vacancies quickly, collecting rent on time, limiting the turnover, and controlling the expenses. Although our manager's compensation that first year increased by $1,600 in extra hours and incentive bonuses, our net profit increased several times over that, easily justifying the increase.

Maintenance:

On any project 15 to 20 years old or older, you can expect to spend 7% to 15% of annual gross to keep the project in good repair. The key to keeping this cost down is not to do any less, but to spend less to get it done. This can be accomplished in many ways, and again we can use the Village Apartments as an example.

(1) Painting. If you expect to get market rents, you need the building to look attractive and well maintained. Due to the size of the project and the need to accomplish it rather quickly, I put the job out to bid. The results were predictable. The bids differed by as much as $8,000. In my experience as a property owner, this wide range is typical and illustrates the very reason you need to have expensive maintenance items bid by several companies. In this case, after interviewing the lowest bidder and determining that he intended to do everything that I required, he was awarded the job. Obviously, the savings involved was well worth my time and effort.

Ordinarily, when the painting just involves a small scale job, paying a handyman an hourly rate is the quickest and least expensive way to get the work done. However, sometimes a flat rate per apartment, say $150 or $200, can be arrived at that saves you major fluctuations in cost from unit to unit.

Since painting is an ongoing job at any apartment complex, it often pays to negotiate a discount price between 10% and 25%, for paint from your supplier, and to keep a supply on hand at the apartment property.

(2) Floor Covering. In my experience, getting a carpet company to replace carpeting for a flat price per room or apartment is the least expensive and most satisfactory way to get this work done on an ongoing basis. On the other hand, many handymen are capable of laying vinyl, purchased by the owner or manager. Doing this, the savings can be 40% to 50% of what a contractor might charge.

(3) Plumbing, Heating and Electrical. This is an area where it is occasionally necessary to hire a professional, usually at rates of $30 to $50 per hour. However, there are often many tasks that a handyman for $6 to $10 can handle. Many handymen can handle such tasks as repair of leaky faucets or pipes, replacement of air conditioning units and repair of faulty switches or outlets.

(4) Carpentry. There are a multitude of items that a handyman can often handle. Items such as

repair of doors, windows, screens, and even replacement of tub surrounds or other finish work in the interior such as paneling or molding. When one is available, utilize a handyman, rather than a carpenter who typically charges $15 to $20 per hour.

Property Taxes:

This is an area where you might assume that whatever the tax is, you are stuck with it. This can be a costly assumption. Again, let's take the Village as an example. Shortly after we closed escrow we were advised that our property was being reappraised. That invariably means that taxes will be increased. We took the initiative and responded that the property taxes had not been decreased during the past several years during which time the property had experienced deferred maintenance, rents had declined, and the value of the property had in turn declined. Although they were not inclined to reduce taxes, as property values had recently started going up, we were successful in freezing our tax at the old rate for the next three years. In the fourth year, in an effort to catch up, they proposed a whopping increase of 70%, to nearly $20,000. After contacting an attorney/ accountant specializing in appeal of property tax increases, we were able to get the increase reduced to about half the amount proposed. At the end we had spent a couple of thousand dollars making our case, but the savings over those first four years of nearly $11,000 made it very worthwhile. Not to mention the thousands we would save in future tax years.

Obviously, such appeals can save you thousands in taxes at the time of appeal and many more thousands in future years. If you are unsure of pursuing such an appeal yourself, most major cities have professionals, usually accountants or attorneys, who will handle your appeal for a fee.

Other Techniques To Increase Income and Expand Wealth:

(1) Vending Machines. Often the addition of vending machines can provide additional income, with no capital expense. The typical soft drink or snack machine can add $25 to $50 to your income per month. Normally, your only requirement is to provide the space and an electric outlet to hook into; the distributor provides the machine and services it. Besides adding a few dollars to income, you provide a desirable service to your tenants.

(2) Washers and dryers. If you have enough tenants to support it, the distributor will put in new or used washers and dryers at his expense, service them as needed, and split the proceeds with you. In the case of the Village, we negotiated with the distributor to

double the number of washers and dryers, and make improvements in the laundry, at their expense. As a result, many of our 40 tenants used the laundry more, and instead of receiving $50 to $75 per month, our share grew to $185 to $225 per month.

Garage/Carport, Parking Spaces or Storage:

Sometimes it's possible to charge extra for certain items that you already have, but which you may not have enough of to provide to every tenant. Because they are desirable to certain tenants, they are willing to pay extra for them. Some examples: A garage can often be rented for $50 to $150 per month, a carport or extra parking space for $10 to $15 per month or a storage locker or small storage room for $5 to $25 per month.

Space Conversion:

Often, space exists in an existing building that can be converted to a more profitable use. A good example of this was found at the Village Apartments. A large room of approximately 700 square feet, formerly the common area recreation room, had fallen into disrepair and was now used for storage and a repair shop. Since it appeared that we might be able to convert it into a one bedroom apartment rather inexpensively, we investigated with our handyman and a plumber and electrician what it would cost to convert it. Since the room and some electrical and plumbing already existed, we were delighted to learn that for approximately $10,000 we could create a one bedroom apartment and a small shop with a separate outside entry. We figured that after we threw out all the accumulated junk the balance could be stored in a portable storage building costing about $500. We felt that we could rent this new one bedroom apartment for about $400 per month, therefore returning our investment in a little over two years. Thereafter, the extra income of $5,000 per year would be nearly clear profit. In addition, since such a unit new would be worth $20,000 to $25,000, we would also be adding $10,000 to $15,000 of equity to our wealth.

Other opportunities for conversion may present themselves that are simpler and less expensive.

Years ago we purchased a single family home that had a large family room with its own bathroom added off the back of the house. Since the property was zoned residential with up to two units per lot permitted (R-2), we purchased the property with the intent of converting the family room into a studio apartment.

It cost us about $2,500 to install a combination sink, stove, refrigerator, add a separate electric meter, close the entry from the main house, paint and install new carpet. We were able to rent the studio for $200 per month and recover our investment within one year. Thereafter we enjoyed the extra $2,500 per year and in a few years, when we traded the property up, received an additional $12,000 in price because of the studio we created.

Management As a Key Element of Building Wealth: The manager of the property is such a key element of profit, that we need to look at what that relationship might be. The typical owner of four to six units will also be the manager/handyman, thereby saving that expense and increasing the profit. But as you get into eight to twenty units, you will need a part-time manager on site. Depending on the capabilities of the manager, he or she may take care of the grounds, clean, paint or make minor repairs, show and rent apartments, collect rents, handle renter complaints, and arrange for subcontractor work to be done when necessary.

Normally this on-site person or couple will get a percent of their rent free plus an hourly rate of pay for extra repair or cleaning they do. Generally a value of 4% to 6% of gross rents is what you expect to give in rent reduction and/or wages.

If you choose to have a management company totally handle the property for you, as an absentee owner you can expect to pay the management company another 4% to 6%, or as high as 10%. Most management companies will still require an on-site manager, so that expense will normally not be eliminated.

On-site managers who are alert can make you money. Frequently they can save you money on buying material or other services reasonably. They almost always save you money on things that they are able to do that avoids the necessity of hiring outside contractors.

Sometimes they are able to make you even more money with their observations or suggestions. They often know when rents can be raised on certain units and when a general increase in rents can be accomplished without increasing vacancies. And after a while, they get a feel from the market as to when larger deposits can be required.

An alert, cost conscious manager can be a significant wealth building factor.

Key Points: Building wealth through good

management is just as important as buying the property for a favorable price and on terms that are advantageous. Virtually every area of expense can be analyzed and will usually make some contribution toward increasing income.

Because of the ongoing requirement to maintain and improve the property, the availability of a handyman on-site — unless you intend to do this yourself — is another key element that must not be overlooked.

Another key element of expanding income, and therefore wealth, is the technique of developing other income sources. Vending machines, parking/garages, storage, space conversion may all be additional sources of income and wealth.

Whatever management arrangement is made, because the abilities of that person are so critical to the profitable operation of a rental property, that person, company or couple should be very carefully selected.

PART IV: YOUR OWN BUSINESS

Chapter 11: The American Dream

Most of us, when we think of wealth, envision large real estate holdings, fancy cars and jewelry, or large sums of money in stocks or bonds. To the surprise of many, a recent survey by the market-research firm, Phoenix-Hecht (as reported in the magazine, Inc. 53-55) "found that of 163 millionaires surveyed, 74% owned their own businesses, and 60% were still working." Although their average annual income of $137,000 was not huge, the big money was tied up in their companies. And even though owning your own business won't assure millionaire status, it obviously helps. The point I wish to make is that owning your own business is an attractive wealth building alternative that is often overlooked.

Some "self-styled" experts would have you believe that building an equity in a business should not be a major goal. They contend that it should not distract from the higher priority of creating cash flow, earnings, and that the satisfaction and lifestyle of owning their own business is enough for most owners. I strongly disagree, even though it is true that an owner must continually focus on the profitability of the business. Since the typical private business will sell for two to five times earnings — and more if the business can be taken public, the value of your equity can be substantial. Since this equity could eventually become a major part of your retirement funds or estate, I think emphasis on building it should be stressed as a major benefit of owning a business. In my own case, even though my first business sold for under $50,000, fifteen years later the business that I retired from brought me nearly $1,000,000.

The thought of being your own boss, of running your own company and making profits beyond just wages has a tremendous appeal to many. This is more noticeable as people become increasingly dissatisfied with their jobs. I believe that a person who has prepared himself to go into business, who selects the right business, and who has the right business plan and sufficient resources and talent to implement it, will succeed.

Let's talk about the preparation and the qualifications necessary to go into business. By way of illustration, the first business that I owned was an employment agency. Although I had never worked in an employment agency, I had dealt with agency representatives who sought to do business with the manufacturing company for which I was an employment manager. Also my background in college included courses in business and personnel management.

Although these qualifications were important and added to my credibility, the real key to my success in the agency business was salesmanship. I needed to sell employers on our service, to get them to list their job orders with our agency and to sell them on the idea that the fee paid was worth it. This I found to be the most critical skill. I have since concluded that most businesses require some skill in selling, and even though I did not have this experience going in, I was successful nonetheless due to the fact that I was outgoing and confident that the service we offered was superior. The point I wish to make is this: Although it is important to be well suited and well qualified for the business that you're attracted to, it is not necessary to be specifically experienced in that business or to have every qualification. That is with the proviso that you are open to learning and at least have an aptitude that will allow you to learn on the job or utilize outside help in acquiring the needed skill.

There is another way to reduce the risk of not having all the qualifications needed for you to feel comfortable with owning a particular business. If you were to purchase a franchise, for instance, it is customary for the franchisor to provide you with a certain number of weeks of training. Better than that, if you were to purchase a "going business," you could require that the owner stay on for 30, 60, or 90 days or longer as part of the purchase agreement. And in some instances the previous owner will even request to be allowed to stay on for six months or even a year or more for his or her own reasons. In any event there are books, seminars and school courses available on nearly every subject that a person might feel they need in order to fill in their background for a particular business.

The other two considerations that prevent many people from owning their own business is fear of failure and the financial risk one takes in investing in business. Again these are very real risks, but they can largely be overcome by the approach you take in going into business for yourself. The typical person thinks in terms of starting a business from scratch. If, however, you are as risk adverse as I am, you will avoid the uncertainties of a new business for the "track record" of proven sales and profits that an established and successful business can provide. In the next chapter we will cover just that, the specifics of Buying a Business.

There is still one other way to own a business, or at least part of a business. Most financial advisers will recommend an investment strategy of buying shares in a business rather than direct ownership of a business of your own. They contend that the risk of direct ownership is greater, that the liquidity is far less, and that by buying growth stocks you can still experience growth similar to what you might achieve if you owned your own business. Although these assertions are generally true, there are compelling reasons for some investors to own their own business:

[1] Owning stocks, particularly growth stocks, is not without substantial risk. Buying an existing business, one that you control, can be a secure investment.

[2] Owners of stock who choose to use leverage can borrow up to 50% of the value of the stock, but face a margin call if the stock declines substantially in price. On the other hand the owner of a business who buys with a down payment of 20% to 30%, has even greater leverage of 70% to 80%. Similarly, additional leverage is created by the financing of buildings, equipment and vehicles. Overall, this amount of leverage in a successful, growing business can increase your return on investment tremendously over a period of time. This will be illustrated with specific examples in the next chapters.

[3] It's true that liquidity is much greater for owning stocks than it is for owning a business. However, when you receive income from a stock or sell a stock for a profit, you have created a taxable event — unless it's in a tax deferred account. On the other hand, your own business can grow in value, year after year, with no tax consequences. For instance, if earnings are plowed back into the company in the form of additional equipment, advertising or work force, and this results in increased sales volume and makes the company more profitable, you have increased the value of the company without creating a taxable event. This is preferable to taking excess profits in the form of wages, reducing this amount by the taxes owed, and then investing what is left in the company. This, unfortunately, is essentially what you are doing when you invest in stocks.

Most successful businesses will grow at least at the rate of inflation, approximately 5%, and many more at 10% to 15% or higher. Whatever the rate, this is a major benefit of owning a business. This increase in value, whether due to internal growth or just inflation, will not be taxable until such time as the business is sold.

Key Points: Owning a business of your own can have many advantages, not the least of which is the satisfaction you can experience as you build the business and add to your wealth simultaneously. To better insure your success, you need to find a successful business for which you are well suited, although not necessarily well experienced in. Buying an existing, at least modestly successful business is the best way to reduce the risk of owning your own business. There are numerous ways to fill in your background and "bring you up to speed" to insure that you will be an effective manager, once you become an owner.

Surveys have shown that the majority of millionaires own their own businesses. This points up the desirability of owning your own business for another reason that is often overlooked. Beyond the satisfaction of owning your own business, the tax sheltered, equity growing nature of a profitable business represents an extraordinary wealth building alternative that we will explore in the following chapters.

Chapter 12: Buying a Business

Since buying the right business at the right price is extremely important, let's go through the necessary steps. First of all, we are assuming that you have evaluated your own personality and found that you would be a good fit for successful ownership of a business of your own. And secondly, you've analyzed your experience, skills, interests, and determined what type of business suits you best. If you have any serious doubts about the suitability of your personality, or experience to successfully run the business of your choice, I suggest you pick up a copy of Snowden's book, <u>Buying A Business</u>, (38-57) which offers you a systematic method of making such a self evaluation.

As you begin your search for an existing business, keep in mind the rationale of why you would seek an existing business rather than start one of your own. If you buy a business that has been successful for a number of years, and there has been no major change in either the business climate or the personnel of that company, then as the new owner you should be similarly successful. However, for this to be true, you must satisfy yourself that certain other requirements have been met:

[1] We have already mentioned the question of your own suitability for the business. Now you must ask, do I have sufficient management talents and experience in this particular business to run the business as effectively as the present owner? If the answer is yes, fine. If the answer is no, you must arrange the necessary training to overcome this deficiency or else pass on that particular business opportunity.

[2] Is there any pattern of downturn in the sales or profits of the company? If so, you must be confident that you can overcome such problems. Some of these problems are as follows: A competitor coming out with a better product, service, or price; costs increasing at a faster rate than sales due to salary increases; the high cost of replacing obsolete equipment and increases in the cost of material or advertising.

[3] Certain financial information must be obtained and analyzed, and your accountant can help you with this one. You will need to determine that the cash projected to come in each month is sufficient to cover all costs associated with operating the company. This includes the monthly payment that you owe after the down payment, a reasonable salary for yourself, and contingency funds for the unexpected.

If you find that all requirements can be satisfied or that whatever problems that have been revealed can be overcome, you have a reasonable expectation of being similarly successful and have, in all likelihood, found the right business.

Before we get into the procedure for buying an existing business, I think you should recognize that there is still one other option available for reducing risk. That is the purchase of a business franchise. Although this may be less risky than to start your own business from scratch, I would avoid most franchises. According to syndicated writer/ consultant, Paul Talenko, (C-3), "at least one-third of all franchises fail in the first four years, more than the failure rate of all business start-ups in general." (As reported in San Diego Union-Tribune 5-8-96.) Courtesy Scripps Howard News Service.)

Although there are many solid franchisors that could merit your consideration, I still feel strongly that owning your own independent business is still the best way for most people to be in business. There are a number of very good reasons for this:

[1]   Being entirely in business for yourself allows you to be fully independent and call your own

shots. A franchisee is expected to follow certain policies and procedures mandated by the franchisor. Plus is subject to periodic inspection and/or review by franchisor management.

[2] A franchisee is typically contractually bound to pay five to ten percent or more of the gross receipts to the franchisor in the form of a franchise fee. This is money right off of the top that will reduce your net profits by a similar amount. Of course this is in addition to the "up-front" fees that you will be required to pay for the privilege of becoming a franchisee in the first place.

[3] Remember, what you are buying in most cases is not an existing, proven, profitable business. What you are buying is simply the opportunity to go into business, and permission to use the franchise name and procedures. There is no guarantee that your franchise will be successful or even profitable from your standpoint.

[4] It takes time to build a business, any business. Day one in a start-up business or franchise, you will have already invested a lot of time and money up to that point, but will only be able to guess as to how many dollars will come in that first day, month or year. This means that your break-even point might be 90 days to a year or more away. In the meantime your existing capital could be used up, you might need to go to the bank for an additional loan, or possibly you will need to draw on your own savings until such time as the business becomes profitable.

Contrast these uncertainties with those of a successful business that you have purchased. From a review of the yearly profit and loss statements and monthly records of sales, income and expenses, the approximate income, expense and net profit can be determined in advance. This allows you to plan ahead, and to know in advance what additional capital might be needed, and probably equally important, to sleep well nights.

[5] Another major limitation to the ownership of a franchise is much less apparent. People truly in business for themselves can add a product or service, expand to additional locations, and when the time comes, sell or leave the business to anyone they choose and on whatever terms they wish. Every one of these actions, in a typical franchise situation, would either require approval of the franchisor, be rejected outright, or require payment of additional fees to the franchisor, if permitted.

Assuming that I have soured any appetite you may have had for owning a franchise, you are now ready to begin your search for an established business. A good place to begin is with a Business Opportunity Broker in your area. They will be listed in the yellow pages, but you can get a feel for the individual brokers and some of the businesses that they have listed by reading their ads in the Business Opportunity section of the want ads in any of the large newspapers circulated in your area. You can also get a feel for the type of businesses being offered, and often the price and terms.

Your first contact with the broker will usually result in your needing to identify the type of businesses you are potentially interested in, the price range, and the amount of cash or down payment that you can readily come up with. On the other hand, you will want to know what type of businesses the broker has listings for that could be of potential interest to you.

Initially, you will want to know price and what is included with it and terms of the sale. The reasons for selling, how profitable the business is and what is included in the price are important questions to ask. Be aware that the right business might be the very first one you inquire about, but this is not very likely. Realistically, for certain types of businesses, it might be months or even years before that particular type of business comes on the market.

Keep in mind that you have a dual purpose here. It isn't just to find the right business, it's also to get to know as much as you can about a cross section of similar businesses, and specifically the typical profits, prices and terms asked for other businesses that may interest you. Information such as this can be invaluable in helping you to evaluate various businesses offered and how they stack up overall against the business that you ultimately target to buy.

Be forewarned that the broker will be eager to sell you a business, any business. His commission is typically ten percent of the selling price and will be paid by the seller whom he represents. Although you could offer a broker a finder's fee to find you the right business, you should only consider this approach if you still have not found the right business after several months of searching. Also, don't overlook the ads placed by private individuals advertising their business in the newspapers, periodicals, and especially trade publications.

You will typically be asked to make a down payment of 20% to 30% of the purchase price.

However, this percentage is negotiable, along with the number of years that the seller will be willing to carry the balance. The carrying period will most often be one to five years.

Expect the asking price to be 10% to 20% more than the seller actually expects to get and, in some cases you can negotiate an even lower price. Prices of businesses are typically based on a multiple of the earnings of the business before taxes. That figure might be as little as one or two times earnings for a young or below average company. On the other hand, four or five times earnings might be realistic for a long established, highly profitable company. Brokers, trade associations, small business appraisers, and certain accountants are a good source for finding what multiples are typical for the kind of business you are seeking to buy.

Once you find the business that appears to be right for you, a number of questions need to be answered. Critical among these is, why is the business being sold? Some of the answers or reasons that would be positive and probably would not affect the future earnings of the business are these:

1. Retirement

2. Illness or death of the owner or manager

3. Undercapitalized but profitable and lacking sufficient capital to expand

4. Any compelling reason that necessitates the owner's relocation to a different geographic area.

Some reasons that would be potentially negative are as follows:

1. Loss of one or more key employees

2. Loss or impending loss of a major client, subcontractor or supplier

3. Declining sales or profits

4. Major expenses or taxes or notes due that have been deferred; major equipment or machinery that is due for replacement

5. Loss or the foreseeable loss of a critical facility, land, or equipment lease

Granted, many of these items will require some serious digging on your part, by your accountant or attorney, but you must know the nature and extent of these "red flag" items. Making an offer contingent on interviewing certain key employees, clients or suppliers is one of the best ways to get at the facts if the records don't tell the whole story. Of course a review of all accounting and other business records should be an automatic contingency that you will insist on.

You must be especially cautious when the owner gives no reason for selling, or at least no plausible reason. In other words, "If the business is so good and so highly profitable, why is it being sold?" If an acceptable answer is not forthcoming, you must dig until you find the real reason or simply pass on what is likely to be a problem business.

The primary tools you will need in order to evaluate and value the business and its present profitability, is an up-to-date profit and loss statement and a balance sheet. This is where your accountant can be very helpful in determining if you have all the pertinent information concerning what you are buying. Any claim by the seller that his profits are substantially higher than those shown - in order to avoid taxes or otherwise — should be disregarded and, in most cases, further consideration of the business terminated. Also, where the financial statement includes the owner's personal expenses: cars, trips, meals, etc., intermingled with business expenses, the statement should be recast to reflect only actual business expenses. This will tend to increase earnings, but legitimately.

Large one-time receipts, such as insurance or deposit refunds, or excessive salary or bonus payments should be factored out also. Your accountant can be very helpful in doing so and projecting realistic earnings for the future. The seller should provide you with the past three to five years of financial statements, and his own projection of profits for the coming year. Preferred, of course, would be audited statements. However, for unincorporated businesses, the owner's personal income tax filings could be analyzed for several years back in order to verify the income claimed by the seller.

Once you and your accountant have done all you can to verify past income and expenses, and the reality of the seller's projections for the future, there are a few more steps that you can take to insure against misrepresentations by the seller and to avoid paying more than the business is really worth:

[1] Base the price you pay for the business on a multiple times the average earnings over the past two to five-year period rather than just the most recent year, which is customary.

[2] Establish a conservative price for the business with a provision for an earn-out. Under an earn-out provision, the price for the business might be increased by a certain amount if the earnings are in line with the owner's projections or greater. This or the price may be reduced if the earnings are less than the owner's projections. An example: The business is to sell for $300,000, $150,000 to be paid initially and the remaining balance of $150,000 paid over the next two years — based on yearly earnings of at least $80,000 or more. Or, in the event that earnings are less than $80,000, the price of the business would be reduced to $250,000 and payments over the final two years would be reduced to $100,000 total.

[3] One of the simplest ways to offset any misrepresentations or inequities caused by the seller is to buy the business on time — ask for credit rather than pay all cash. Let's assume you made a down payment of 20% of the purchase price and your contract calls for payment of the balance in monthly installments over a three-year period. One year later you discover a discrepancy of $12,000 that should contractually be the obligation of the seller. You now have the leverage of the unpaid balance to ensure that you are credited with that amount. Had you paid cash for the business, you would have had little leverage in forcing a resolution if the seller had balked at reimbursing you.

Often in your initial call to a seller or broker through the want ads, they will stress how much the business is grossing, or the high value of the property or other assets owned by the business. Frequently this is just a dodge to hide the fact that the earnings are low or that the business is actually losing money. Since you are initially interested only in what the business nets or what the before-tax earnings are, don't waste your time with these people unless you are looking for a turnaround opportunity. Even then, most of these businesses are so overpriced and the seller so inflexible that you will still be wasting your time.

Having said that, let's examine a turnaround opportunity. When I was 30 years old and ready to leave big industry for a business of my own, I found just such a business — an employment agency — through a business opportunity broker. Although the business, priced at $10,000, was not priced that much over the value of the assets, the actual earnings, I later determined, were slightly negative — contrary to the claims of the broker. It was owned by a couple, one who worked in the business full time and the other just part time. Although the business was growing and had a good reputation, after two years they were selling. This was due to a situation where the husband was unable to quit his job and come in full time as planned because the wife wasn't realizing wages out of the business as yet, even though the business was just starting to turn a profit. In addition, they had lost their inexpensive office lease in an older building which was scheduled to be replaced by a new high-rise building soon.

We estimated that the office furniture and equipment alone were worth $6,000 to $7,000. Even though we would have some expense of moving the offices to a new location, we decided an offer of $6,500 was fair. We knew that it would likely be six to twelve months before I could draw any salary from the business and they were made aware that $3,000 down and the balance over a one year period was the best that we could offer and still have enough cash left to operate the business and pay our personal expenses for six months or more.

To our great surprise, they accepted. This meant we had purchased the physical assets of the business and paid nothing for the going business itself, including: three productive employees, the necessary city and state licenses, forms, stationery and everything necessary to continue the business. Before we made the offer, we had located brand new offices in a nearby building which the owner was willing to rent to us for not much more than the rent in the old building. We accepted, contingent on escrow closing on the employment agency.

Meanwhile, another pleasant surprise awaited us. The sellers still had several thousand dollars in earned commissions to be collected and they preferred that we do it through the business. After some discussion of the billing procedures, follow-up calls needed and the handling of receipts, it was agreed that we would receive 25% of all their receipts collected and assume no liability for those we were unable to collect. This added to our cash flow significantly in the early going without requiring us to invest anything other than our time.

All in all, we had made a very good deal for ourselves. Although our approach was rather risky in light of the business being just at the break-even point, my background and some long hours enabled me to start drawing a small salary within four months and a struggling business soon became a solid, profitable business.

And even for the sellers it was not a bad deal. Had they been forced to vacate their building they would have had to sell their furniture and equipment at liquidation prices (less than we paid) and also would have been forced to act as their own collection agent or turn it over to a collection agency for 40% to 50% of the accounts collected.

One element of purchasing the employment agency that I didn't go into was the involvement of my accountant and an attorney. Any offer to purchase should always be subject to an inspection of the financial records of the business, the business premises, and the physical assets and inventory. Permission should be given to interview any key employee, subcontractor, supplier or key account. Before you sign any agreement it should be reviewed by your attorney. In addition, your attorney can protect you with warranties or other clauses against any misrepresentation by the seller, whether intentional or not. For example, inclusion of an "offset clause" allows you to offset the amount of your monetary injury against the balance owed the seller, if it becomes necessary, without the expense of going to court. Say that an unpaid tax lien against the property was discovered after the property was sought. The amount of the lien, your injury, could be deducted from the balance of the note owed to the seller.

Key Points: Buying an existing business can be your first step toward independence and accumulating wealth. Knowing yourself, your temperament, and essentially your suitability for owning a business of your own, should be carefully evaluated before you take this step. Also, an objective inventory of your experience and skills should be taken in order for you to determine what type businesses you might be best suited for and have the best chance of succeeding in.

Part of the process of finding a suitable business is screening out owners who are selling for the wrong reasons and discovering changes or hidden losses that could affect the price or future profitability of the business.

Since the underlying assumption here is to buy an existing business in order to reduce risk, the possibility of purchasing a franchise is also examined. Unfortunately, there are many limitations to operating as a franchise owner as opposed to being your own boss in your own business. These limitations, plus the initial cost and ongoing burden of franchise fees, should be carefully considered before considering entering business as a franchisee.

The techniques employed in searching for an existing business, the way you evaluate it against other businesses, and the resources you employ in reaching a buying decision, are crucial to buying a business in which you can be successful. Since prices and down payments are all negotiable, the better deal you are able to conclude, the better return on investment you will be able to realize. Because net profit is the most important yardstick by which businesses can be measured, one must insist on reviewing profit & loss statements, balance sheets and supporting records in order to determine the true worth of the business.

Use of an accountant and attorney is absolutely essential to insure that you actually get what the seller claims you are getting. This is important in buying the business, and for protection against any misrepresentations that may be discovered after you own the business. Use of brokers, appraisers, want ads and trade journals are useful in establishing typical prices and terms for comparing many different kinds of businesses.

The following chapter will profile two businesses that I have owned and operated, to give you a picture of the wealth building potential of investing in a business of your own.

Chapter 13: Actual Business Profiles

The profiles that follow demonstrate how a small investment in a business can lead to a buildup of significant wealth within that business. These are actual business experiences of my own, businesses that I bought and operated myself, the results of which contributed greatly to the financial well being that my family and I now enjoy.

EMPLOYMENT AGENCY PROFILE:

Dates: Purchased mid 60's and sold 7 years later.

Purchase Price: $6,500

Down payment: $3,000

Terms: 1 year

Sale Price: $35,000 less commission = $31,500

Typical Gross: $100,000+ Typical Net: $28,000*

   ***including owner's salary plus profits**

Sales Price Multiple: 1.25 times earnings before tax

This profile, even though reflecting prices 25 to 30 years ago, is nonetheless revealing. What the profile illustrates is that with an investment of $6,500 initially, and a net sales price of $31,500, I was able to realize an annual compound rate of 25% on my investment over the seven-year period. This does not take into account that the business paid me a very nice salary/profit during the period of my ownership after the start up period, plus provided me with a car, group insurance and an expense account. These statistics clearly indicate that this investment outperformed most investments I could have made in the stock market plus it provided me with the independence of my own business and the salary/ profits that exceeded what I would have made had I remained at my previous job.

To further illustrate the possibilities in buying a business of your own, and how it might perform as an investment over a longer period of time, let's take a look at another business that I owned for a period of 15 years. This construction and remodeling company specialized in the reconstruction of condominium complexes of typically 150 to 500 units, and ultimately became a testing source and consultant to the industry. The success of the company began in the early 1980s when we identified a particular niche in the industry. We began to realize that there was a considerable market in rebuilding at that time, particularly in restucco and recoating the exterior of buildings. We were continually being asked to give estimates to repair such buildings, which were mostly apartment and condominium complexes that had exterior finishes of Rescon, a stucco substitute produced by the Johns-Manville Company, that was failing badly and the subject of numerous law suits. Within a few years, this phase of the business expanded to the extent that we became the experts for the estimate and repair of all types of construction defects, and a good business became an excellent business and investment.

Identifying a particular niche comes about primarily by being sensitive to the needs or changing needs of customers and potential customers. It's a matter of keeping informed through word-of-mouth and business and industry publications of changes or trends in your industry. And when a person thinks they've spotted a niche, they must be willing to commit both time and money to be able to capitalize on it.

The Construction Company Profile will give us still another idea of the potential and the advantages of an investment in a business of your own.

CONSTRUCTION COMPANY PROFILE:

Dates: Purchased early-70's and sold 15 years later

Purchase Price: $33,000

Down payment: $12,500

Terms: 18 months

Sale Price: $800,000 (sold privately)

Typical Gross: First 5 years $800,000 to $1,500,000
Last 5 years $2,000,000 to $5,000,000
Typical Net: First 5 years $50,000 to $100,000*
Typical Net: Last 5 years $150,000 to $250,000*
***including owner's salary & not including maximum contribution to owner's pension fund**
Price Multiple: 4 times earnings before tax based on 5 yr. avg.

This profile reveals that with a down payment of $12,500 and the balance of the purchase price paid out of the business, at a sales price of $800,000, over the 15-year period I realized a compound return on my initial investment of more than 30% annually. Also, in the later years, through our corporate defined benefit plan (pension plan), the corporation contributed the maximum benefit to my plan annually (typically $80,000 to $90,000) and, proportionate to their salary, other key employees as well. Obviously it would be an extremely rare investment on Wall Street that would do this well over an extended period of time. Although the taxes on such a sale are brutal, by spreading payments over a four or five-year period, the tax bite can be reduced somewhat. On the other hand, over the 15-year period, the growing value of the business was sheltered from taxes. In addition, the considerable sum in my pension plan was accumulated tax deferred, and will continue to grow, tax deferred, as a rollover into my private IRA.

Now let's examine how a similar investment, if made today, might fare over the next 25 years. I've used the approximate average of the two initial investments that I made in the two businesses of $6,500 and $12,500 respectively, rounded off to $10,000, and took an average of the two compounding rates for those two businesses, or 27 percent. The result allows us to peer into the potential future of a business of your own.

YOUR OWN BUSINESS
Compounding Rate - 27%

Age	Investment	Year End	Year End Value
30	$10,000	1	$ 12,700
35	-	5	33,308
40	-	10	109,153
45	-	15	366,240
50	-	20	1,191,446
55	-	25	Ending Value 3,936,343

Your first reaction to this surprisingly large ending value may be disbelief. Or, if not, how then is this possible? Part of the answer is that it takes a dedicated owner/operator with some particular talents for that kind of business, and a business that makes sense and enjoys some success early on. This is the reason for buying an existing, healthy business.

The other part of the answer is leverage and the compounding effects of staying with a successful business investment over an extended period of time. As was mentioned earlier, buying a going business with 20 percent to 30 percent down allows you to leverage 70 percent to 80 percent of your investment, plus the additional leverage you create by financing equipment, inventory, or any other need of the business that increases profits.

Granted, every business is not going to be as successful as the two businesses that I profiled, and a few will simply not make it at all and go out of business. And yet you can hardly pick up a newspaper or business magazine without learning of another "rags to riches" success story. The <u>San Diego Union-Tribune</u> recently reported where "Mac" McQueen an engineer, and Robert Deane a salesman, back in 1964, put up $350 each and went to work in their home garage. They believed that a sensing device for reporting whether a well was operating or not was needed by the oil industry, and they set about designing and manufacturing one. As their product gained acceptance and they diversified, for the first several years their company doubled in size every year. Today that company's, (Fluid Components') annual sales are in excess of $20 million.

Another interesting article that I found instructive recently appeared in <u>Fortune</u> (236 pages) magazine. And I quote, "What is now the nation's No. 1 bookseller was born in 1971, when Barnes & Noble founder and CEO Leonard Riggio bought a single stagnant Manhattan store. Today it's a 937-store chain. Why? Credit two profound insights into what consumers want and a readiness to make big bets on that understanding." Also significant was that this was an established business without the uncertainties of starting a new business. This allowed the CEO, with profits already coming in, to be creative and focus his efforts on expanding the business through the use of leverage.

One of the all-time great success stories is that of Sam Walton, who started in 1950 with one Ben Franklin store. Again, the basis of this success begins with the purchase of a single successful store. Later in 1962 he opened his first Wal-Mart store with a determination to sell his employees on a philosophy of efficiency and service to the customer, at discount prices (<u>Current Biography Yearbook</u> 281 pages). His success was such that his stores rang up sales of over $40 billion by 1991, his net worth made him one of the richest men in America. Notably, part of his successful formula for running a business was to locate big stores in rural areas and give great latitude to his store managers in developing their own marketing schemes and running their own stores.

So, while the accumulation in value pictured in the previous profile might have seemed impressive before, it pales in comparison to many of the business success stories reported here and in your daily newspaper or magazine publications.

Key Points: An analysis of actual business profiles illustrates dramatically the huge profits and eye popping possibilities for accumulation of wealth that are available in a business of your own. This is particularly true if an existing business is purchased, and especially true if that business has profits, or at least great promise of profits.

Most such successful businesses have two things in common, talented owner/managers, and owners, confident of their abilities and willing to use an ample amount of leverage to "grow the business." Characteristics that these owners often share are that they are reasonably risk tolerant, passionate about their company, and display a certain vision or ingenuity. They have good timing, or drive, or often it's just plain hard work that allows them to succeed grandly, whereas less inspired or less talented owners just get by.

The wise use of leverage contributes greatly to the ability of a company to expand sales and profits, and therefore, the value of the business. As in any investment, leverage plus the compounding of an investment in your <u>own successful business</u>, over an extended period of time, can in this instance, add immeasurably to your wealth.

PART V: TEN INVESTMENTS TO AVOID AND WHY

Chapter 14: Beware of These Wealth Busters!

Warren Buffet, probably the best known self-made billionaire investor in the world, makes the point that there are only two rules you need to follow in order to amass great wealth. Says Buffet, "Rule number one is, don't lose money. And rule number two is, never forget rule number one!" My own experience in the investments covered in this chapter is that the risks of losing money far outweigh the potential gains.

The greatest danger most investors face is not a low percentage return on their investment but that they will get a low percentage of their investment returned to them. Such is the wealth busting potential of investments I list in this chapter. Investments in most limited partnerships lead this list of risky, even dangerous, investments. Limited partnerships are business ventures designed to give the investor, the limited partner, an opportunity to participate in profits with limited risk. The general partner manages the business in exchange for a management fee and a percentage of the profits, if any. The limited partner in turn receives a larger percentage of the profits and any losses are <u>limited</u> to the amount invested. This quotation from Ken and Daria Dolan's <u>Straight Talk on Your Money</u> newsletter nearly says it all: "Only 17% of all people invested in limited partnerships ever get their original investment back again, much less get a <u>return</u> on their investment." (Nov. 93, page 5) Let's take a closer look at this list of "Wealth Busters."

    1. LIMITED PARTNERSHIPS: Limited partnerships cover many areas of investing but probably best known are those in real estate, oil and gas, and leasing. The way these offerings are typically packaged, the investment is structured to include 10% to 15% front loaded fees (sales commissions and promotional fees). The general partner totally controls the investment and receives annual administrative and management fees for his involvement. The limited partner's liability is restricted to the amount of his investment and he may receive a tax deduction of anywhere from 10% to 100% of the amount of his investment depending on the way the investment is structured. In addition, a major part of any net profit or capital gain goes to the limited partner. One of the problems with most such partnerships is that only about 80% to 85% of the investor's money is put to work for him initially, so in effect he starts out with 15% to 20% loss. This, coupled with the fact that the general partner, upon whom you are depending to represent your best interests, often may have other interests that conflict with your own. Let me sight one of my own experiences with a real estate limited partnership.

2. REAL ESTATE LIMITED PARTNERSHIPS:

Back in the 1970s, a financial planner, whom I had become acquainted with through a friend, highly recommended a particular real estate partnership. Because of the partnership's successful track record with previous offerings over a seven-year period, I invested. Their previous record showed that they had been successful in buying apartment rental property at favorable prices, improving these properties and their values, and then selling the properties in three to five years for a nice capital gain. During the holding period they had been paying the limited partners (LPs) an 8% to 12% annual income on their investment.

During the first year of my investment the income checks came in on time and everything seemed to be fine. In the second year income checks were delayed and then stopped. It seemed that expenses had been continually going up for no apparent reason. Investigations by LPs were begun and lawsuits filed. It turned out that over the years the general partners had set up their own subcontract carpet, drapery, cleaning and other remodeling companies. In a position to charge our apartments whatever they wished, they drained off the cash flow slowly but steadily, causing the properties to go into bankruptcy. Because the general partners had paid too much for the properties when originally purchased for the LPs, the equities that we thought we would recover out of bankruptcy were non-existent after attorney fees.

This unfortunately is not an exception in the real estate field, as nearly every other type of LP that is sold suffers from similar limitations or potential conflict of interest problems. Aside from my own experience, I have read of a great number of such cases and learned from friends of their own numerous horror stories. Because so many of these LPs are structured such that they grossly over-compensate the general partner and grossly under-protect the limited partner, the unwary investor should be forewarned that this is the most hazardous area of investing that he or she is likely to encounter.

3. OIL AND GAS LIMITED PARTNERSHIPS:
Again, from my own experience and judging from the numerous negative reports appearing in daily newspapers and financial publications as a whole, this can be a very risky area of investment. Back in

the early 1980s when oil and gas investments were hot, I invested in two different oil and gas limited partnerships. The first one was highly recommended by my brokerage firm, E.F. Hutton, now known as Smith Barney Shearson. The second one was top rated by one of the industry's most widely acclaimed analysts, who had issued his in-depth reports and then recommended the best of that year's offerings.

E.F. Hutton's LP offering ,a combination exploratory drilling program (risky) coupled with production drilling (supposedly conservative) returned to me less than 40% of the amount of my original investment. After several years of decreasing oil production and falling oil prices, the LP filed for bankruptcy and the remaining 60% of my original investment was lost.

The second LP, the industry analyst's top recommendation for production oil and gas wells, got off to what I thought was a great start. Nineteen of twenty wells dug went into production.

The first year's income was on target, and then the demise of another LP began. Some wells simply didn't produce enough oil or gas and had to be capped. Others, the cost of recovering the oil or gas became too great and they were abandoned. As cash flow decreased, certain productive wells were sold off to keep the LP solvent. After ten years, my total cash return on this so-called conservative investment was less that 25%, in other words — a loss of 75%.

What went wrong? And why do even conservative investments of this type so often turn out this way? One part of this answer is always the same: as investors, we are at the mercy of the syndicator and the general partner. This is because they are too optimistic in their projections of future oil and gas prices, and they conservatively project what the expenses will be. They also project what oil and gas reserves are in the ground and how much will be recovered — typically way overstated. More risks are the up front costs of such offerings — costs that comes out of your investment — plus the inflated price often paid for the better oil and gas prospects. The broker gets his commission, the general partner gets his management fee and you get what's left. Unfortunately what typically results is that even with your tax deduction, plus any cash paid back to you, what you receive in total is less than the amount that you invested to begin with.

4. LEASING LIMITED PARTNERSHIPS: Although these types of LPs have generally fared better than others, there have still been many problems. High priced products such as airplanes, computers and portable buildings are typically what are packaged. Again you are at the mercy of the general partner. Questions you must ask are: What are the up front fees? Is the partnership paying too much for the products they intend to lease? Are the leases in place, or are you being offered leases they hope to place? Even if the income stream claimed is enough to pay you 12% to 15% annually on your investment, is the residual value of the product, after the lease period is over, sufficient to return the amount of your original investment? Or will obsolescence set in, preventing the recovery of assets as projected by the general partner? These are all tough questions, and it's even tougher to get reliable, unbiased answers before you invest.

So what it generally boils down to is this: you must rely on and have considerable faith in, the general partner. Imagine the feelings of investors who originally felt reassured that their investments, with Prudential as a general partner, were as "Solid as a Rock." Back in the early and mid 1980s, before the lawsuits began, Prudential-Bache Securities Inc., sold partnerships which invested in wide ranging ventures including energy, real estate, aircraft and even horses. Now, with thousands of lawsuits pending and with hundreds of millions of dollars at stake, even these investors have found that picking a solid general partner is no guarantee. The Wall Street Journal has since reported that for some of these partnerships, where $8 billion had been invested, investors had so far received payments of only $3 billion plus residuals. (Greg Steinmetz and Michael Siconolfi; 12-1-93).

Some of these investors, all part of an oil and gas class-action suit against Prudential, were considering a settlement that some of their attorneys estimated at no more than one cent to five cents on the dollar. (San Diego Union-Tribune, Don Bauder 1-24-93).

1 believe that what we can conclude from all the evidence is that investments in limited partnerships have generally fallen far short of investor expectations. And since avoiding loss is a key element of building wealth, and since there are so many other superior investment alternatives available, limited partnerships generally represent unacceptable risk that should be studiously avoided.

5. VARIABLE ANNUITIES: Although this investment is not high risk, the investment does have certain pitfalls that can cause your overall return to be very poor. Since it is a vehicle that offers a tax deferred return, including typically some life insurance and a variety of mutual fund investments, the public has generally viewed this investment as conservative and it has enjoyed great popularity accordingly. The problems with this complex investment vehicle are its actual and potential costs. Costs vary from company to company, but all will typically charge fees similar to these: A small fee to set up the annuity contract plus an annual fee of ` 1/2% – 1% for the mutual fund expense. There is also an annual expense for insurance of 1% - 2%. The real "wealth buster," a surrender charge of 5% - 10% is charged if you surrender in the first year, typically declining by 1% a year thereafter. And then if you should withdraw your money any time before you are 59-1/2 years old, the government socks you with another 10% penalty for early withdrawal.

Analysts Ken and Daria Dolan (Straight Talk on Your Money, October '93) have estimated that because of the fees involved in investing in an annuity with an insurance company, rather than in a regular mutual fund, it can take 20 years to match performance. For these reasons and the inflexibility of such an investment that essentially locks you in for years, variable annuities should be passed over in favor of other, less costly, and less confining investments.

6. GOLD AND SILVER: During periods of high

inflation, investments in gold and silver bullion, coins, mining stocks, penny stocks and even gold futures become popular with many investors. The reason is generally valid: gold and silver act as a store of value. During these periods of high inflation, when your paper money buys less and less, gold will typically continue rising in value and be worth more, in relation to paper money, and therefore retain its purchasing power. If an economic or political catastrophe were to develop, gold and silver, because of its intrinsic value, would still retain its value and be acceptable for barter, whereas paper money might become nearly worthless. Because of this ability to act as an inflation hedge, many people, including myself, are willing to hold a small amount of gold and silver simply as a sort of disaster insurance.

The problem is, gold or silver bullion doesn't earn interest, it doesn't create wealth, and just to hold it can even cost you storage fees and insurance. There are, in addition, other related investments that should be discussed.

7. RARE COINS: Unless you are a dealer or just want the satisfaction of owning such coins, forget it. Because of the great expertise required and the long periods of depressed markets, even many of the dealers go bankrupt just trying to hold on. I have owned a variety of rare coins since the mid 1970s when it was profitable to do so, with gold selling at nearly twice what it sells for today. Over the years I've bought and sold thousands of dollars in coins without realizing a significant profit. As a hobby it's great. As an investment, it's over-hyped and has totally under-performed investor expectations for nearly two decades.

8. STOCKS (PRECIOUS METALS): Because stocks tend to rise even faster than bullion in periods of high inflation, they can be big money makers in that climate. But unfortunately, the reverse is also true. In times of declining inflation, these stocks can drop so fast as to make a major dent in the value of your portfolio for years to come. Not the sort of investment that offers the steady, low risk return that can be expected from other types of equity investments.

9. PENNY STOCKS: These stocks are so speculative that I've noticed that even knowledgeable newsletter writers often recommend that you buy eight or ten different stocks in hopes that one or two might become successful. These are often shares in mining companies that hope to raise enough money, and furthermore hope to be successful in finding sufficient gold or silver to market for a profit. Then if their costs to produce are not too high, they hope the price of gold or silver will be sufficiently high to allow them to make a profit. In an investment such as this, based on a lot of "ifs" and "hopes," the risks far outweigh any potential gain that can be reasonably expected. The same is also true of non-mining penny stocks as well.

10. COMMODITY FUTURES: These are contracts to buy or sell a commodity at a specified future time, based upon a price agreed upon today. The commodity could be gold, other metals, hogs, wheat or a number of other items. Speculators in commodity futures can control, or own, many contracts for just the small amount of deposit required. Because of this huge leverage, a small change in market price can double their investment, or if it goes against them, wipe them out. The key word here is speculator. This is an industry so speculative that often even the professionals lose money. Since investing for the long run, without taking losses along the way is our objective, gambling on commodities is best left to the pros.

11. BONDS: Ordinarily, bonds, which are the debt of corporations or government, are considered to be a conservative investment. However, from the standpoint of building wealth and keeping ahead of inflation, they are a poor investment. According to

Ibbotson Associates, between 1926 and 1992 a typical bond portfolio broke even after inflation was subtracted, while growth for Standard & Poor 500 stocks experienced annual net growth of 7%. With a bond portfolio there is some reliability in the set amount of interest you will be paid, and some safety of principal if you buy highly rated bonds and hold them to maturity. But if you should need to sell a bond after an interest rate rise, or after a credit rating service lowers a bond's credit rating, the market price will undoubtedly be down and you could lose money. Also, since you as a bond holder have no equity/ stock ownership in the company, the good fortunes of the company will not be reflected in appreciation in the value of your bond. Should the company falter or fail however, it could default on payment of its debt, which could in turn leave you with a less valuable or even worthless bond.

Despite all of this, high quality bonds can be a regular source of interest income if held to maturity. But inasmuch as they represent no prospect for growth and offer no inflation hedge, as a wealth building vehicle they are a bust and should be avoided.

Key Points: The greatest danger that most investors face is a substantial loss of the principal amount of their investment, not just a low return. One investment of this type that represents the greatest threat is Limited Partnerships. Limited Partnerships are formed to cover ventures like: real estate, oil and gas and leasing — anything from computers to airplanes.

There are a number of characteristics that most of these LPs share: high front loaded fees, inconsistent management and conflict of interest with LPs. There is also the failure in a majority of the programs to even return the amount of the original investment. It doesn't seem to make a difference even when the general partner is a well known, major U.S. corporation. Since avoiding loss is a key element of building wealth, limited partnerships generally represent an unacceptable level of risk.

Variable annuities have become one of the most popular ways for investors to invest these days. This is largely because they offer a tax deferred return and the flexibility to invest in money market or a variety of other mutual funds. Unfortunately, the fees typically charged outweigh the potential value of tax deferral. That plus the onerous surrender charges tend to lock you in, and therefore eliminate much of the apparent flexibility of annuities.

Gold, silver and related investments in coins and mining shares can act as inflation hedges in times of rising inflation. However, gold and silver do not pay interest, they do not create wealth and, as such, they do not merit consideration as wealth building alternatives. As for penny stocks, these highly speculative investments are best suited to those who have the urge to gamble.

Commodity futures are another area of speculative investment best left to the pros.

Bonds, because as they offer no opportunity for growth and offer no inflation hedge — as a wealth building vehicle are, for our purposes, a bust.

PART VI: INVESTMENT ALTERNATIVES FOR THE WEALTHY AND WOULD BE WEALTHY

Chapter 15: "Hands Off" Investing

Once a person has accumulated a substantial sum of money, from whatever source, he may not wish to be involved in the day-to-day management of that money. Fortunately there are reputable companies that manage such funds, companies with excellent track records. I refer to this approach as "hands off" investing, as it allows the investor to put funds into the hands of professional management without the need to participate in the management of those funds.

All such companies are available to investors through major brokerage houses such as Smith Barney, Dean Witter Reynolds and other sources that I will cover as each type of manager is presented for consideration. All such managers are individual companies, independent of the brokerage house that may represent them. In addition, all such managers are followed by companies that report on the results obtained by each manager over one, three, five and ten-year periods. Then these results are compared with those of other, similar type managers, over the same time frames. For each manager presented, I will outline their particular investment philosophy, the results each manager has been able to produce, and what is required of the investor. These requirements, which typically demand an initial investment of $100,000 to $500,000 unfortunately limit availability of this type of manager to the wealthy. However, as I will explain later, there is another avenue that may be available for investors with $25,000 to $50,000 to invest.

C.J. Lawrence

The first money manager I would like to introduce you to is C.J. Lawrence, Deutsche Bank Securities Corporation, managed by Van Schreiber, Managing Director. This firm has been in business since 1864 and currently manages $2.9 billion. Deutsche Bank Group, the parent company, with global financial institution assets of $385 billion, offers sound (AAA) backing (top financial rating). The program that is offered is known as the Premium Growth Equity Portfolio, a portfolio of medium size company growth stocks (much smaller than one of the 30 Dow stocks). These stocks, typically 20 to 30 in a portfolio, are selected on the basis that earnings growth is projected to be at least 50% higher than market averages, and are selected from sectors that are growing faster than the economy as a whole. There are 37 sectors. Ranging from air transportation to computers and medical to telecommunications and finally utilities.

Through the extensive research capabilities of C.J. Lawrence and other select institutions, they first determine underlying, powerful trends in the U.S. economy that provide profitable investment opportunities. Then they determine which are the fastest growing sectors likely to benefit from these trends, and then the specific company/stocks uniquely positioned and able to exploit these trends. The growth character of the portfolio is maintained by adherence to a strict sell discipline. A stock will be sold when it is determined that one or more of these conditions have developed: There is excessive institutional ownership and exposure, the industry fundamentals are deteriorating, or the occurrence of negative earnings surprises.

Depending on client preference, they manage growth equities in two ways: Fully invested, or active asset allocation utilizing the proprietary C. J. Lawrence Market Monitor. Since I consider managing risk an important element of building wealth, I prefer the asset allocation option. This may result in lower returns, but it also provides greater protection against experiencing a negative return for your portfolio in any given year.

Example: In a strong up market the manager may hold 90% stocks and only 10% money market funds, to maximize gains. In a weak or volatile market subject to large loss, the manager may hold only 40% stocks and 60% money market in order to reduce risk.

The annual returns achieved by C. J. Lawrence, Deutsche Bank Securities corporation (CJL/DBSC) are truly impressive. **[See Figure 10]** Figure 10 tells us that returns have ranged from a low in 1994 of 6.40% to a high of 102.15% in 1991. And a compounded annual return of 34.06% was reported for the five years ending in December 1994. Although a terrific return, realistically in my experience the 34% is not likely to be sustained as, with the passing of a greater number of years, such high averages tend to trend down. More impressive to me, from a preservation of wealth and a wealth building perspective, are the positive returns in 1987, 1990 and 1994. These were all difficult years for the market with the majority of money managers reporting negative returns for those years. And yet, in spite of the negative market environment, and in spite of being invested in growth stocks which are generally considered more risky, C. J. Lawrence was able to achieve positive returns of 7.94%, 25.92% and 4.40% respectively. Of course, such outstanding results did

FIGURE 10

Performance
Premium Growth Equity
Assets Under Management: Over $300 Million *

Annual Returns (%)

	CJL/DBSC Premium Growth Equity Composite	Russell 1000 Growth Index	S & P 500 Index
1987	7.94%	5.31%	5.18%
1988	50.73%	11.27%	16.50%
1989	30.93%	35.92%	31.44%
1990	25.92%	-0.26%	-3.20%
1991	102.15% *(the highest)*	41.16%	30.54%
1992	12.45%	5.00%	7.69%
1993	47.80%	2.90%	9.99%
1994	6.40% *(the lowest)*	2.66%	1.33%
3/31/95	2.47%	9.52%	9.73%

* Assets as of 12/31/94
Please see disclosure

Compounded Annual Returns

	CJL/DBSC Premium Growth Equity Composite	Russell 1000 Growth Index	S & P 500
1 Year	11.33%	17.61%	15.59%
3 Years	22.19%	8.52%	10.56%
5 Years	34.06%	12.18%	11.42%
7 Years	30.61%	14.04%	13.39%

as of 3/31/95

PIPER

• Ranked second for 5 year performance out of more than 200 growth equity managers, evaluated by PIPER* at the end of 4th quarter 1994

* The PIPER reports are compiled by Rogers Casey & Associates Inc

C.J. Lawrence
Deutsche Bank Securities Corporation

not go unnoticed. The Piper Report, compiled by Rogers Casey & Associates Inc., ranked CJL/DBSC second for five-year performance out of more than 200 growth equity managers evaluated at the end of the third quarter of 1994 (C.J. Lawrence, Prospectus 1-95). Obviously, such an outstanding equity manager should be considered by any investor who doesn't wish to manage his own portfolio and who can meet the requirements.

Unfortunately, one of the requirements is that an initial investment of $500,000 is the minimum required to open an account. But the fee required to manage this account is a modest one percent annually. You may inquire further about such a managed account by contacting a major brokerage house or C. J. Lawrence directly:

C. J. Lawrence
Deutsche Bank Securities Corp.
1290 Avenue of the Americas
New York, NY 10101
Phone: (800) 334-1898
Fax: (212) 468-5379

For those who are interested, but can only invest $25,000 to $50,000 initially, there is one other possibility. Some of the brokerage houses, such as Smith Barney, are willing to establish a clone account. This is essentially a clone of the C. J. Lawrence Premium Growth Equity Account, just on a smaller scale.

Essentially the account follows C. J. Lawrence's lead as to what stocks to buy and sell and the percentage of cash versus equities to be maintained in the account. This account would be held at your own brokerage house and reported on by them. The fee would be higher for such an arrangement, typically 2% to 3%.

Another possibility for the investor who wants diversification in his or her stock holdings is a managed account in foreign stocks. Whereas the U.S. market was 80% of the world market 25 to 30 years ago, today it is estimated to be less than 40%. In addition, stocks in Europe and the Far East are generally cheaper than U.S. stocks. Still another consideration is that foreign stocks have some tendency to do well in certain years when the U.S. market has performed poorly. Case in point, in the stock market crash of 1987 the S&P 500 gained only 5.3%, whereas the EAFE index (European, Australia and Far East) gained 24.9%. More recently, in 1994 the S&P 500 gained 1.3%, while the EAFE was up 8.1% (Dean Witter, Access Report 12/92, 12/94). The point is, if you don't want to have all your eggs in one basket, an investment in foreign stocks is one way to diversify and potentially increase your overall return.

One of the finest services that I know of in this area, and one that has been recognized by The Wall Street Journal, Barron's and reporting services such as Nelson's Directory of Investment Managers, and Money Manager Review, is Brandes Investment Management. In the Spring issue, the 1993 Money Manager Review (Brandes Prospectus, Jan. 93) reported Brandes to have the best five year return of 12 international managers with an average annual return of 26.14. Brandes' return was also rated as that with the least risk of these surveyed.

Brandes Investment Partners, Inc. International Portfolio

In looking at individual stocks to invest in, Brandes seeks to build wealth through the systematic identification of real value. This involves finding companies that are financially strong, with measurable worth. When its stock is selling at a price well below its worth, they buy it. In time, the market will recognize this value and the price will rise. When the stock is no longer undervalued, it will be sold.

This approach recognizes that the more undervalued a stock is, the greater potential for profit. And just as important, the greater the gap between price and value, the greater the margin of safety. Value investing requires patience as value investors tend to think in terms of three to five year market cycles, the time typically required to realize a substantial profit.

The overall results for Brandes International portfolio, as reported by <u>Nelson's Directory of Investment Managers</u> at the end of 1994, were still impressive. In spite of being down 3.2% for 1994, a particularly tough year for foreign stocks as well as U.S. stocks, Brandes still returned an annualized return of 14.85% for the last five year period, and 22.71% for the ten year period. In light of the proven low risk, low turnover approach of Brandes, I still consider this manager one of the best in the business. It's interesting to note how diversification paid off in the 1993 and 1994 years. Funds invested in the S&P 500 for these two years returned a total of 11.3%, whereas funds invested in Brandes International realized a total return of 37.64%.

The requirements to invest in Brandes' International is a minimum initial investment of $100,000 and an annual management fee of 2% to 3% including Brandes' and the broker's fee. The typical portfolio will contain 20 to 30 stocks and will be fully invested except for 5% to 10% in liquid funds in money market accounts. In order to invest with Brandes, you need to go through a broker such as Dean Witter Reynolds or any major brokerage house. You will receive monthly reports on your account from the broker and quarterly reports from Brandes. For further information on Brandes or on any of the managers presented in this chapter, your main library may have a copy of <u>Nelson's Directory of Investment Managers</u>. Or contact Brandes directly:

> Brandes Investment Partners, Inc.
> 12750 High Bluff Drive Suite 240
> San Diego, CA 92130
> Phone: (800) 237-7119; Fax: (619) 755-0916

The last money manager I would like to bring to your attention is quite different from the first two. Schreiner Capital Management does not seek value, exceptional earnings growth or stocks with certain levels of capitalization, nor does it even invest in individual U.S. or foreign stocks. What Schreiner does is invest in sectors of the stock market, each represented by certain mutual funds. Using quantitative data, they determine which of 12 sectors are currently "in favor" (out-performing the market), or "out of favor" (under-performing the market).

The 12 sectors of the market include: Air Transportation, Health Care, Energy Service, Food & Agriculture, Technology, Leisure & Entertainment, Chemicals, Computers, Financial Services, Telecommunications, Utilities, Retailing. These 12 sectors are each represented by Fidelity's (Mutual Fund) Select Industry Sector Funds, a unique family of specialized funds created in 1981. The following is an overview of how Schreiner manages these funds.

Schreiner Capital Management, Inc. (SCM):
Here's how it works. Every business day, Schreiner Capital Management determines which of the 12 sectors is currently "in favor" and which is "out of favor." If one or more sectors is "in favor," they allocate 1/12th (8.33%) to each sector "in favor" and the remaining assets are placed in the safety of the money market (cash account). The entire process is repeated daily. Money is re-allocated as each sector moves in-favor or out-of-favor. In general during a "bull market" 50% to 75% or more will be invested in sectors, and during "bear markets," less than 50% will be invested in sectors.

This systematic approach offers two advantages. First, with lower than average exposure to the market, it offers significantly less risk than typical equity, or stock portfolios. Second, by investing in sectors with superior relative strength, it creates the potential for excellent returns. This system recognizes the need for diversification, but only among the strongest sector stocks. They believe that diversification in a broad range of stocks doesn't necessarily reduce risk — it simply encourages mediocre returns.

SCM's investment discipline is 100% quantitative. They don't rely on subjective interpretations of news, earnings reports or analysts' reviews of forecasts. Their focus is entirely on fact, not opinion. This investment formula has proven its reliability in tests that have been conducted since the inception of sector funds in 1981. SCM states in their prospectus that their "discipline is a sound strategy that works best for investors seeking growth, who wish to avoid the high costs and risks associated with individual stock ownership." I would agree — although SCM's statement is too modest. They have an excellent record for achieving outstanding growth, while minimizing risk better than just about anybody. According to <u>Money Manager Review</u>, Summer of 1993, in a survey of 634 equity managers, Schreiner Capital Management, with an annualized return of 19.29%, ranked in the top 10% for highest return over a five year period. In the same survey, over the same five year period, SCM was rated Number 1 for

Risk-Adjusted Return. **[See Figure 11]** This tells me that they are able to produce significantly greater long term returns at much less risk than most stock portfolios. This is exactly the type of investment that allows compounding to work best, producing low risk/high returns that can build the tremendous wealth that few investors ever realize.

SCM's performance has been consistent. In 1990 when the S&P was down 6.6%, SCM was up 14.1%. In 1991, 1992 and 1993 when the S&P was up 26.3%, 4.5% and 7.1%, SCM was up 30.6%, 13.6%, 14.2%. In the tough market year of 1994, while the S&P lost 1.5%, SCM managed a gain of 8.8%, out performing most money managers.

I learned of SCM through Carnegie Asset Management, a company affiliated with the Wall Street Digest. Carnegie handles client relations and administration, for which it receives a fee. The entire fee is 2.5% for the first $100,000 — the minimum account acceptable. Above $100,000 it is 2.25% and a declining percentage over $250,000. Since SCM uses Fidelity Sector Funds, there is a 3% up-front load fee. However, if you are already invested in Fidelity, some or all of this fee can be waived. Or, if you are not invested in Fidelity, SCM will waive their management fee until you are reimbursed the full 3%.

Top 65 Equity Managers Sorted by 2 Year Return

From a Survey of 634 Equity Managers as of Mar. 31, 1993

Advisor's Name	Min. Acct Size (000's)	One Year Return	Three Year Return	5 Year Return
1 Onehaus Capital Mgmt. Small-Cap.	3,000	28.34	43.46	36.71
2 Gardner Lewis Asset Mngmnt.	1,000	16.77	40.37	36.45
3 Kopp Investment Advisors	250	43.59	38.80	29.87
4 Duncan-Hurst -Medium Cap	10,000	21.09	36.17	27.90
5 George Blumarr/Growth	1,000	25.37	32.24	27.32
6 Mark Asset Management	2,000	23.96	21.15	26.18
7 Rayner Associates	500	29.24	30.31	26.01
8 Lynch & Mayer-Mid. Cap.	10,000	29.47	27.94	25.46
9 American Advisors Corp.	200	6.88	23.19	24.75
10 Berger Associates Investment Mgmt	1,000	-15.71	27.34	24.58
11 Neumeier Investment Counsel	3,000	26.58	21.94	
12 Amerindo Investment Adv.	250	7.94		
13 Oak Associates	5,000			
14 Invesco Trust Company				
15 Pension Management				
16 Janus Capital				
17 Peregrine Capital				
18 Fred Alger Management				
19 Turner Investment				
20 Provident Investment				
21 Chancellor Capital				
22 Friess Assoc. inc.				
23 Target Investors inc./Co...				
24 J. W. Burns & Company				
25 Quasar Capital Management				
26 Global Financial Management				
27 First Wilshire Securit. Mgmt.				
28 Cambridge Equity Adv. inc.				
29 Cohen Davis & Manta inc.				
30 Greenville Capital Mngmnt				
31 Nicholas-Applegate-Growth				
32 Emerging Growth Mgmt, Co. Eq				21.42
33 Aegon USA Inc.			19.52	21.15
34 General American Investors				
35 Pennaus Asset Mgmt, inc.		11.01	18.62	21.08
36 Pacific Century Adv. inc.-Sm/Co	5,000	-1.00	20.99	21.01
37 Arnhold & Bleichroeder Corp.	5,000	26.41	19.93	20.99
38 Coen & Denemore investments	5,000	2.73	14.05	20.99
39 PVG Asset Management Corp.	250	17.52	25.49	20.88
40 Private Capital Management	500	32.87	19.31	20.77
41 Northern Trust Company	5,000	15.70	21.51	20.75
42 Cheswick Investment Co.	1,500	-19.70	15.99	20.39
43 Trinity Invt. Mgmt. Corp./Sec.Ptx	5,000	34.02	18.58	20.16
44 W.P. Stewart & Co.	1,000	12.08	22.02	20.08
45 Kalmar Investments inc.	250	10.21	19.66	18.99
46 Simms Capital Management	500	4.19	20.06	19.8
47 Townsend Group Invt.	100	-6.88	13.06	19.9
48 McHugh Associates inc.	1,000	7.95	18.01	19.79
49 Denver Investment Advisors	10,000	10.68	23.51	19.76
50 Statistical Sciences inc.	500	15.89	17.79	19.72
51 Moody, Aldrich & Sullivan	500	32.41	20.81	19.37
52 Norman L. Yu & Co. inc.	250	2.67	18.58	19.36
53 Schreiner Capital Management	100	13.23	18.58	19.23
54 Sands Capital Management Inc.	400	6.52	17.76	19.23
55 RCB Trust Co.- Small Cap	2,500	13.38	21.70	19.22
56 Phoenix Investment Counsel	20,000	15.86	19.71	19.11
57 Zazas Sarais & Associates inc.	500	17.97	21.05	19.13
58 F. Martin Koenig Advisors	500	7.46	22.93	19.01
59 Florence Festmngton inc.	5,000	23.76	20.03	18.86
60 Meridian Investment Company	10,000	13.83	17.99	18.86
61 Voyageur Asset Management	5,000	11.37	17.42	18.78
62 Pacific Income Advisers	250	16.95	18.44	18.77
63 Marathon Investment Mngmnt.	100	22.13	18.56	18.73
64 Robertson Stephens invt.	10,000	-11.36	15.22	18.54
65 Barings America Asset Mgt.	10,000	14.84	18.15	18.53

Top 65 Equity Managers Sorted by 2 Year Return/Risk

From a Survey of 634 Equity Managers as of Mar. 31, 1993

Advisor's Name	Gross/Net Of Fees	Reporting Method	ADR Standards	1 Year Return Rate
1 Schreiner Capital Management	Net	Unaudited	N/A	4.25
2 Aegon USA Inc.	Gross	Representative	No	4.23
3 Neumeier Investment Counsel	Gross	Unaudited	Yes	4.11
4 Private Capital Management	Net	Unaudited	Yes	3.84
5 F. Martin Koenig Advisors	Gross	Represent.	Yes	3.88
6 Pension Management Co.	Gross	Model Portfolio	No	3.56
7 Pennhaus Asset Mgmt, inc.		Representative	Yes	3.49
8 Trinity Invt. Mgmt. Corp./Sec.		Unaudited	Yes	3.48
9 Marathon Investment		Representative	No	3.33
		Unaudited	No	3.23
		Unaudited	No	3.18
		Audited	Yes	3.18
		Unaudited	Yes	3.03
		Representative	Yes	2.90
		Unaudited	Yes	2.97
		Audited	N/A	2.58
		Quoted	Yes	2.81
		Quoted	Yes	2.79
		Unaudited	No	2.79
		Portfolio	Yes	2.75
		Representative	Yes	2.73
		Representative	No	2.70
		Representative	No	2.58
		Representative	Yes	2.58
		Representative	No	2.57
		Representative	No	2.56
		Representative	Yes	2.54
		Audited	Yes	2.49
		Representative	N/A	2.45
		Model Portfolio	No	2.42
31 ... Management	Net	Unaudited	No	2.29
32 Gardner Lewis Asset Mngmnt.	Net	Model Portfolio	No	2.30
33 PVG Asset Management Corp.	Gross	Unaudited	Yes	2.30
34 Janus Capital	Net	Unaudited	No	2.30
35 Provident Investment Counsel	Gross	Representative	Yes	2.38
36 Duncan-Hurst -Medium Cap	Net	Model Portfolio	No	2.31
37 General American Investors	Gross	Unaudited	Yes	2.30
38 George Blumarr/Growth	Gross	Representative	Yes	2.26
39 Barings America Asset Mgt.	Gross	Unaudited	N/A	2.17
40 McHugh Associates inc.	Gross	Representative	Yes	2.12
41 Kalmar Investments inc.	Net	Unaudited	No	2.10
42 Berger Associates Investment Mgmt	Net	Unaudited	Yes	2.08
43 Mark Asset Management	Gross	Unaudited	No	2.08
44 Denver Investment Advisors	Net	Representative	No	2.04
45 Sands Capital Management inc.	Gross	Representative	Yes	2.01
46 Coen & Denemore investments	Gross	Unaudited	Yes	1.96
47 Emerging Growth Mgmt, Co. Equity	Gross	Model Portfolio	No	1.94
48 Friess Assoc. inc.	Gross	Model Portfolio	Yes	1.93
49 Peregrine Capital-Smal Cap.	Net	Unaudited	Yes	1.93
50 Oak Associates	Gross	Representative	Yes	1.92
51 Nicholas-Applegate-Growth	Gross	Unaudited	No	1.88
52 Kopp Investment Advisors	Net	Model Portfolio	Yes	1.87
53 Fred Alger Management Sm. Cap.	Net	Unaudited	Yes	1.82
54 RCB Trust Co.- Small Cap	Net	Audited	Yes	1.78
55 Global Financial Management Co.	Net	Unaudited	Yes	1.75
56 Cambridge Equity Adv. inc.	Net	Model Portfolio	Yes	1.74
57 Greenville Capital Mngmnt	Net	Unaudited	Yes	1.58
58 Pacific Century Adv. inc.-Sm/Co	Gross	Unaudited	No	1.58
59 Target Investors inc./Compos.	Net	Representative	Yes	1.54
60 Amerindo Investment Adv.	Net	Unaudited	Yes	1.54
61 Townsend Group invt.	Net	Representative	Yes	1.53
62 Cheswick Investment Co.	Net	Unaudited	No	1.53
63 Robertson Stephens invt.	Net	Representative	No	1.39
64 Norman L. Yu & Co. inc.	Net	Representative	No	1.37
65 First Wilshire Securit. Mgmt.	Net	Unaudited	No	1.32

FIGURE 11

Schreiner Capital Management's
Sector Investing
Ranked Number 1
for Risk-Adjusted Return
for the Five Year Period ending March 31, 1993
According to *Money Manager Review*

Also Ranked in the Top 10% of 634 Equity Managers
for *Total Return*

For further information you may call Carnegie Asset Management at (800) 966-7693 or Schreiner Capital Management at (800) 351-0268.

In the next chapter, we will examine a totally different type of "hands off" investment, one that does not require any of your money. It is an investment approved by the government — that allows you to fund entirely with tax dollars.

Key Points: "Hands off" investing allows a person to hire a proven professional management company to carry the load of investing in stocks. Minimum investment requirements range from $25,000 to $500,000.

Each money management company reviewed offers a unique approach to investing in the stock market, but most important, they all share a risk adverse approach.

C.J. Lawrence offers investors an opportunity to invest in medium size growth stocks in the fastest growing sectors of the U.S. market. They reduce risk by utilizing an asset allocation model. Returns for the past five years averaging 34% places them second in a group of 200 equity managers.

Investors with $25,000 to $50,000 may consider a clone account with one of the major brokerage houses such as Smith Barney if the $500,000 minimum is out of reach.

One way to diversify one's stock holdings is to invest in foreign stocks. One of the most widely recognized management companies in this field is Brandes Investment Partners.

Their approach is based on buying below a stocks worth and holding it for a three to five year period in order to realize substantial profit. The worth of this approach is reflected in their returns. For the five year period ending in the Spring of 1993, of 12 international managers reporting, they were number one with the lowest risk and an average annual return of 26.14%.

Minimum investment required is $100,000, but you may be able to set up a clone account through your broker for a lesser amount.

An entirely different approach is offered by Shreiner Capital Management. Utilizing a broad range of mutual funds, 12 sectors of the market are invested in depending on whether they are "in favor" or "out of favor." By investing in sectors with superior relative strength to the market, they are able to achieve outstanding returns. And with lower than average exposure to the market they reduce risk significantly.

Chapter 16: Put Your Taxes To Work — Uncle Sam's Wealth Building Gift

The problem most of us have in common is that after we pay our federal and state income taxes, there isn't much left to invest. Fortunately, under the Tax Reform Act of 1986, the federal government has provided us with a rare opportunity to spend our tax dollars wisely, by investing for our own benefit in low income housing with tax dollars that would otherwise be a dead loss to us. What the government has done is to encourage the construction of housing for low income families and the fixed income elderly by offering us tax credits to invest in or build such units.

This is not generally known because the government treated it as a temporary program until making the program permanent in 1993 — in the meantime causing both investors and syndicators to be wary. Now that it has permanence and a solid track record has been established, it has lost most of the stigma of limited partnerships.

One may use tax credits to offset up to $25,000 of active income from employment or business. This means that if you are in a 28% tax bracket, up to $7,000 in taxes could be diverted to an investment in low income housing. If you are in a 36% tax bracket, up to $9,000 could be diverted. When I say diverted, I mean that the $7,000 or $9,000 that you would have spent on taxes will be saved for investment instead. In other words you'll make the investment of up to $7, 000 to $9, 000 and then it will be refunded when you file your tax return. Either way, these dollars can continue to be invested, year after year into an investment in low income housing that will help others, while helping you to accumulate an equity in real estate.

The typical investment in low income housing is available as a limited partnership, and there are several companies to choose from that offer such programs. Each sponsoring company becomes the general partner. Normally you will either make a one time investment of a minimum of $5,000 or you will make a total investment of $25,000 to $50,000 with four to six installment payments ranging from $4,000 to $10,000 each, allowing you to fund all or most of the payments from your tax credits each year over the four to six year period. This type of information is presented in the company's prospectus. Generally speaking, you will receive tax credits of about 150% of your investment, and these credits typically will be spread over a ten year period.

In an investment of this type that I made personally, [See Figure 12] I committed to making six annual installment payments varying from $3,500 to $12,760 each totaling $50,172, and received federal and state tax credits of $5,000 to $10,000 each, payable to me over a ten-year period totaling $75,000. The way it worked out, over the first six years I received tax credits of $45,723, covering all of my installment payments except $4,449. At that point my installment payment obligation stopped as the $50,172 was fully funded, but my tax credits will continue at approximately $5,900 per year for the next four years. This will save me an additional $23,680 total in taxes that I can invest elsewhere.

Now let's look at the overall potential results of such an investment, assuming the property is sold or refinanced after a mandatory 16 year holding period required by the government. **[See Figure 12]**. Figure 12 illustrates that an initial investment of $50,172 would be worth $160,853 [**] seventeen years later, (assuming annual appreciation\ inflation of 4%). This is a tremendous result when you consider that if we had just gone ahead and paid our $50,172 in taxes over a six year period, we would have had zero dollars to show for it.

FIGURE 12

INVESTMENT OVERVIEW

COLUMBIA HOUSING PARTNERS XVIII	Columbia Financial 1200 5th Avenue Seattle, WA 98164

SUMMARY OF FORECASTED PER UNIT LIMITED PARTNER BENEFITS
45 LP UNITS

Schedule A-1

INDIVIDUAL INVESTORS NOT ABLE TO UTILIZE PASSIVE LOSSES

BENEFITS FROM OPERATIONS:

Year	Capital Contribution (A)	California Credit (B1)	Federal LIHTC (B2)	Total Tax Credits (B1+B2)	Annual Net Investment (E)	Cumulative Net Investment (F)	Credit as a Percentage of Payment (Annual)	Credit as a Percentage of Payment (Cumulative)	Passive Loss (C)
1989	3,500		251	25	3,249	3,249	7.17%	7.17%	(4,506)
1990	10,500	5,002	5,363	10,365	135	3,384	98.71%	75.83%	(7,493)
1991	12,760	5,002	5,859	10,861	1,899	5,283	85.12%	80.26%	(6,823)
1992	8,725	5,002	5,859	10,861	(2,136)	3,147	124.48%	91.13%	(6,378)
1993	8,580	1,667	5,859	7,526	1,054	4,201	87.72%	90.47%	(7,233)
1994	6,107		5,859	5,859	248	4,449	95.94%	91.13%	(7,198)
1995			5,859	5,859	(5,859)	(1,410)		102.81%	(5,489)
1996			5,859	5,859	(5,859)	(7,269)		114.49%	(4,905)
1997			5,859	5,859	(5,859)	(13,128)		126.17%	(4,447)
1998			5,859	5,859	(5,859)	(18,987)		137.84%	(4,987)
1999			5,608	5,608	(5,608)	(24,595)		149.02%	(5,521)
2000			495	495	(495)	(25,090)		150.01%	(5,111)
2001						(25,090)			(4,562)
2002						(25,090)			(4,866)
2003						(25,090)			(5,389)
2004						(25,090)			(4,966)
2005						(25,090)			(4,407)
TOTAL	50,172	16,673	58,589	75,262					(94,281) ***

[handwritten: initial investment — total of installments]

[handwritten: Total passive losses can offset other LP gains]

FORECASTED PER UNIT SUMMARY OF GAIN, TAX LIABILITY AND TOTAL BENEFITS ASSUMING THE SALE/REFINANCING OF ALL PROPERTIES AT JANUARY 1, 2006:

	SALES PRICE	
	MORTGAGE +$1.00	4% ANNUAL APPRECIATION
PROJECTED CASH FROM SALE OF PROPERTY:	0	103,660
TAX(LIABILITY) BENEFIT FROM GAIN ON SALE:	17,410	(18,069)
SUBTOTAL (G):	17,410	85,591
CUMULATIVE TAX BENEFIT FROM PASSIVE LOSSES:	0	0
CUMULATIVE TAX BENEFIT FROM TAX CREDITS:	75,262	75,262
TOTAL BENEFITS (H):	92,672	160,853 **
LESS ORIGINAL INVESTMENT:	(50,172)	(50,172)
NET RETURN:	42,500	110,681

[handwritten: gain]

[handwritten: total worth — 17 yrs. later]

Considering that it is not only possible, but highly likely in this case and in similar offerings still being made, to recover a $50,172 loss [*](taxes) and add on a gain of $110,681, it may seem almost too good to be true. And as if this were not enough, the government, in order to attract our investment, offers us a bonus in the form of passive losses. Passive losses are those generated in a business in which you have an investment but do not take an active role. Wages or profits from owning a business in which you have an active role, cannot be offset with passive losses. However, these passive losses can be used to offset taxes on passive income from other limited partnership programs such as those involved in property ownership and leasing.

Or if you own income property, income from your own rental units can be offset to the extent that you have current or unused accumulated passive loses available. In my own program described above, I will receive total passive losses of $94,281 [***], receiving $4,407 to $7,400 yearly over a 17 year period. This is more than most programs offer, because it includes state benefits, presently available only in California. However, most programs do offer passive losses of at least 60% to well over a 100% of the amount you invest. Although there is no question that this and similar programs with similar results are available, there are certain precautions you should take in order to achieve the desired results.

First of all, don't make this investment at all unless you expect with some degree of certainty to have sufficient income to create the tax credits needed to fund such an investment for the one to six installments that will be required. Be aware that funds invested in this program will be tied up for at least 15 years, the time required by the federal government for a program of this type to qualify fully for the tax credits.

Although I believe this type of limited partnership to be an outstanding investment, you still need to choose your syndicator/general partner very carefully. Since both public and private programs are available, you need to know the advantages and disadvantages of each. The public programs can be invested in for as little as $5,000 and often offer wide diversification of properties across many states. The private programs are usually less diversified, encompassing just one geographic area such as three or four adjoining states. Also, the private programs typically involve a larger investment — usually at least $25,000 to $70,000, the maximum allowed. On the other hand, most offer installment payments over several years which may allow you to invest each year approximately the amount you would have otherwise paid in taxes.

Whether you choose a public or private syndicator, be sure that the company has been in business five to ten years and has sponsored at least eight to ten low income housing programs previously. The syndicator you will want to invest with will have a verifiable good track record which can be evaluated in the prospectus that must be provided to you. That record, in order to be favorably considered, should reveal consistently high occupancies of the properties averaging 90% or more, experienced property managers on-site and in the headquarter offices, and a spotless record of providing the tax credits projected without any credits being disallowed by the government.

To help you select an experienced syndicator, the following companies are offered. The listing under "PRIVATE COMPANIES" is one that I have invested in myself and with which I have been completely satisfied. The other companies listed under "PUBLIC COMPANIES" are five of the leading companies provided by Phillips Publishing, Inc. in their publication entitled: Taking Advantage of Tax Credits. This publication reviews low-income housing credits and strategy in depth and is available from:

Phillips Publishing, Inc.
7811 Montrose Road
Potomac, Maryland 20854
Telephone: 1-800-777-5005
Refer To: Mark Skousen's,
Forecasts & Strategies
Special Publication Cost, $39.95

PUBLIC COMPANIES:
Boston Capital
313 Congress Street
Boston, MA   02210
Telephone: 1-800-866-2282

Boston Financial
101 Arch Street
Boston, MA 02110
Telephone: 1-800-782-7890

Raymond James & Associates
880 Carillon Parkway
St. Petersburg, FL 33716
Telephone: 1-800-237-4240

The Related Companies
625 Madison Avenue
New York, NY 10022
Telephone: 1-212-421-5333

The Richman Group
10 Valley Drive
Greenwich, CT 06831
Telephone: 1-203-869-0900

PRIVATE COMPANIES:
Columbia Financial
1200 5th Avenue
Seattle, WA 98164
Telephone: 1-206-682-5677

Key Point: Since it is increasingly difficult to find tax sheltered or tax favored investments, low income housing tax credits present us a unique and valuable wealth building opportunity. While we are able to recover tax dollars otherwise lost to us, we are also able to invest these same dollars in such a way that the investment in low income housing becomes a tax shelter. This allows our investment to grow in step with the market and inflation and yet not be subject to personal or capital gain taxes until we sell. And then, if we have not used the passive losses that accumulate with this investment, we can use them to reduce or eliminate entirely taxes on the gain when we sell.

In order to obtain a cross section of programs available and to educate yourself as to variables in each program, I suggest that you send for several prospectuses. Determine which company and offering you feel most comfortable with and best fits your needs, and then get an objective evaluation of the offering and whether it fits your particular tax and financial situation. Because these offerings and the tax considerations are so complex, I strongly urge you to have your accountant or tax attorney assist you in your review before making a final decision.

Don't let the complexity prevent you from investing in this unique tax favored and tax sheltered investment. It truly is a wealth building gift.

PART VII: START-UP TO WEALTH

Chapter 17: What To Do Now

According to a recent study by Merrill Lynch & Company, "People 25 to 44 are saving at a rate that will provide them with only a third of what they will need to maintain their current style of living when they retire ... (Gould C2+)." Although this is cause for concern, I believe it is not too late for anyone who still plans to work at least another 15 to 20 years to accumulate substantial wealth. Whether your goal is to accumulate wealth for your family, for a richer life style, or for your retirement, by starting now it's still within reach.

The first step for those late starters is the same as it for those who start younger: inventory your financial affairs. Your wealth is your home, any other property you may own, your pension fund or IRA, savings, life insurance or stocks, and other income producing assets you own, such as bonds, trust deeds and alimony.

The second step is to determine how much of your income you save now or could save. In other words, how much can you add to your investments on a regular basis? For those who are presently saving little or nothing, I understand. Most of us have faced the same problem. After you pay your regular bills, take care of special family needs and spend a few dollars for yourself, there's nothing left. Tough as it may seem, most people can still save 5% to 10% of their income if they do two things. First, instead of paying all the bills first and then saving what's left, you must give saving a higher priority and pay it first, right along with other bills you are committed to pay. You need not feel guilty about paying yourself first as we all have a responsibility to be self sufficient when we reach our retirement. Beyond that, wealth in later years can also mean greater security for your grandchildren and even your children should they fall on hard times. Secondly, to make savings much easier, a proven method is to have the money come out of your pay check or bank account automatically, before you can spend it. Some individuals find that committing an increase in pay to payroll deductions is one of the least painful ways to save. Others who consistently receive a tax refund annually, raise their number of exemptions so they can sign up for a monthly payroll deduction that will funnel this refund into their savings on a monthly basis, rather than waiting for the annual IRS refund. Whatever the source, a single, one time decision directing that money be deducted from your paycheck or bank account is far less challenging than juggling bills payday to payday, trying to squeeze out enough money to invest.

Now let's go back and look at your financial inventory of wealth. There are two questions that need to be asked: Can you manage the wealth you have more effectively, for greater gain? And do you earn at least the 15% to 20% compounded annual returns produced by all of the wealth building alternatives recommended in this book?

Assuming that there is room for improvement, let's first examine how you might be able to manage what you own better and for greater returns. If you have been fortunate enough to be able to participate in a pension plan with your employer, are you making the maximum contribution that you are allowed to make? If your employer puts in 50% of what you contribute or matches your contribution, that's an impressive first year return of 50% to 100% on your investment. Furthermore, are these funds invested in money market funds at 4% or 5%, or in growth mutual funds or stocks at returns averaging 15% or more annually? Remember, for the long haul, you don't have to play it ultra-safe by investing in money market funds only. You have time to realize the higher returns of growth stocks that will make a big difference in the amount of wealth you will accumulate.

In any event it pays to maximize your investment in either a pension fund or your own IRA. With pension funds these are pretax dollars, and both pension and IRA funds grow tax deferred until you retire. If you don't have a pension fund at work, make the maximum personal IRA contribution each year that you can, $2,000. If you are in say a 28% tax bracket, you are in effect getting an immediate 28% return on your investment because of the tax deduction allowed exempting the contribution from tax.

If you have cash value life insurance, the investment portion is probably earning you 4% to 8% annually in increased cash value. To increase your return, consider replacing the policy with cheap term insurance with a lower monthly premium and investing the cash value and the monthly savings in alternative investments earning 15% to 20% or more as described in this book.

Any other income you may be receiving, from whatever source, should also be invested at these higher alternative investment returns.

If you own your home or other property, consider how you might be able to create additional funds for investment. Often in a home that you have owned for a number of years, your equity is sufficient to consider refinancing. This is particularly true during periods, such as now, when interest rates are down. Often, a new 30 year loan at the lower interest rate will allow you to take thousands out of your home to invest in alternative investments, while keeping your monthly payment at or about the same level. Another option, if you are fortunate enough to already have a low interest first mortgage on your home, is to seek a home equity (second mortgage) loan — sometimes available at rates as low as 7% to 9%. Of course you need to reinvest the funds for a high enough return to make the second mortgage payment and have funds left over to invest. Or, another saving technique is to treat such a loan payment as an enforced savings plan and, in effect, force yourself to save the amount of the payment each month. Then, instead of investing just for income, you will be able to invest for higher long term wealth building returns.

Of course, we shouldn't overlook the fact that owning your own home is, in itself, a wealth building alternative. However, the historical rate of compounding, averaging 5% - or, for the last 20 years, 6% to 7% - just barely keeps ahead of inflation. An individual home, given the right advantages, can appreciate in value at a much higher rate. For instance, a home that is purchased below market price, in a good neighborhood, in a growing community, and is improved and well maintained, can compound annually at 8% to 10% or more. Even a $100,000 home, compounding at just 5% over a 25 year period, will grow to a value of $346,000. This plus the advantage of being able to take a tax deduction for interest payments on the mortgage, including any home equity loan, makes this another wealth building alternative that should not be overlooked.

And finally, if you own land or other negative income property, sell and put your equity and what you save into more productive investments. Or, better yet, trade up — tax deferred — into apartment rental property with positive cash flow.

Now that you have looked at what you own and many of the options available to you, let's look at the wealth building alternatives presented in this book and what you need to do to put one or more to work for you at the higher rates of return available.

[See Figure 13] If you look at Figure 13, it illustrates what $10,000 invested for 25 years in a money market or S&P 500 account would typically be worth, versus the typical worth of the four different

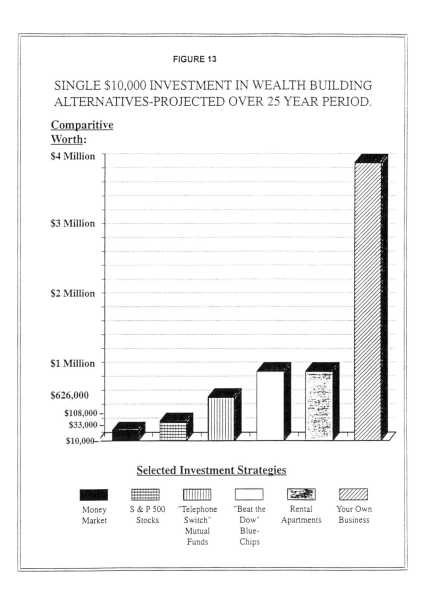

FIGURE 13

SINGLE $10,000 INVESTMENT IN WEALTH BUILDING ALTERNATIVES-PROJECTED OVER 25 YEAR PERIOD.

alternative investments compounding at the higher rates that I have experienced.

The difference is dramatic. The first two, the money market compounding at 5% and the S&P 500 compounding at 10% would be worth $33,864 and $108,347 respectively after 25 years. The four alternative investment values, after the same period, would range from $626,686 for the Telephone Switch Strategy compounding at 18%, to $3,936,343 for Your Own Business compounding at 27%. In between with very solid wealth building compounding of 20% we have Beat the Dow and Rental Apartments growing to nearly $1,000,000.

The conclusion that becomes painfully clear here is that an ultra conservative investment in a money market account, accumulating just $33,864, can hardly be considered a significant wealth building alternative. While, for just a modest amount of risk, as represented in a Beat the Dow strategy or an Apartment Rental investment, highly significant wealth of $953,962 could be accumulated over the same investment period. Obviously then, the choice you make initially in selecting an investment alternative can be extremely critical. On a personal level, the ultra conservative investor could find himself or herself just getting by in later years, whereas the investor who is willing to take at least a modest risk, is much more likely to be able to look forward to a comfortable life and even an early retirement that substantial wealth can bring.

Because Figure 13 also illustrates that as the rate of compounding increases, so does the risk — let's compare the risks. Excluding a money market investment which is almost risk free, an investment in Telephone Switch is the lowest risk. This is due to the fact that you are only in the market when the trend is up, and when the trend is down, you are safely in money market funds. While, at the other end of the spectrum, an investment in your own business has many risks such as how stiff the competition is, the ups and downs of the economy, your ability to retain key employees and key accounts, and the overall profitability of the business. In between we have intermediate levels of risk: because Beat the Dow strategy has you in the market all the time, it represents more risk than Telephone Switch, and yet, because you are invested entirely in blue chip/high yield stocks, the risk is modest. By the same token, Apartment Rentals can also represent modest risk. This is primarily because the strategy is to purchase units that produce enough income to more than offset expenses — with what is left over providing profit and a margin of safety.

There are several other factors to consider before switching any of your present investments into one of the four investment alternatives recommended: time required to own such an investment, the amount of expertise required, and your own temperament.

As to time, Beat the Dow strategy requires the least. Once a year you select either five or ten of the lowest priced, highest yielding stocks in the Dow. At the end of the year, you sell those five or ten and buy the current five or ten meeting the test. It requires very little expertise and is ideal for the investor who wants higher returns but with minimum involvement.

Telephone switch is similar. It requires buying and selling typically one to five mutual funds, on average, only once or twice per year. And if you subscribe to their newsletter, very little expertise is required. This is perfect for the investor who wants to be involved, but with a minimum expenditure of time.

The time required to own or manage rental apartments can vary from a couple of hours per week to many hours if you are inclined to do fix-up work yourself. The number of hours you contribute is largely up to you. For the person who is busy, the fix-up and management can often be performed by an on site manager. For the people who are handy and want to further maximize profit by reducing expenses, their greater involvement can be very profitable. This is also not an investment that requires great expertise. If you make it a point to know the rental market, become familiar with typical rental and house rules and agreements, and keep on top of rent collection and improvements to your property, little more is required in order to be successful. Most owners of rental apartments have full time jobs and donate just the amount of time they find to be profitable. A fringe benefit that you derive from this investment is knowing that you provide renters with a nice place to live at a modest price. Also, you can take some pride in knowing that by improving the property, you've improved the neighborhood.

Your Own Business, as an investment, goes way beyond the other investment alternatives in terms of time, expertise, and personal commitment. Most successful business owners put in 50 to 60 hours a week or more. Most have either some training or experience in the business, or related skills in sales, management, or technical know how. The most successful people are dedicated to their business and will be active in the business for 15 to 20 years or more. In my opinion, unless you are similarly committed, and unless you are prepared to spend at least ten to fifteen years in the business, you will not achieve the exceptional returns that a business investment is capable of producing. By the same token, for those of you with the right competitive temperament and resolve, I know of no greater wealth building opportunity than that represented by a Business of Your Own.

Although I have compared the risks of the various investment alternatives presented, I truly believe that if you follow the approach I've outlined in each chapter, these small risks, can be further minimized. Investors face a far greater threat to their wealth — or potential wealth — by doing nothing. The <u>Wall Street Journal</u> reports that experts say "Individuals take too little risk," argues H. Bradlee Perry, Chairman of David L. Babson & Company. "In the short run stocks are risky. But in the long run they're not ... the trend is upwards." (Clements C-1). According to Ibbotson Associates who has figures since 1926, bonds gained 4.8% a year and Treasury bills 3.7% ... "Barely ahead of inflation, which rose 3.1% during the same period." (Clements C-1). The problem is, unless you as an investor take the first step in setting up some kind of savings plan, or better utilize the assets you already have, the wealth building process of compounding will never be able to work effectively for you. Unless you assume some risk in higher return wealth building alternatives, your investments in money market or CD accounts can be so eroded by inflation that over some time periods your purchasing power, or real wealth, will actually decline.

There is an ancient proverb that says, "The longest journey begins with a single step." I encourage you to take that first step. To start a savings plan if you don't already have one, or to increase the amount if you do. And, if you haven't already done so, to start investing now in one or more of the wealth building alternatives presented that are designed to greatly increase your chances of becoming a successful investor.

In as much as the results illustrated in Figure 13 were based on a single investment of $10,000, for those investors able to invest more initially, or who are able to add two or three hundred dollars more per month, these results could easily be doubled or even tripled.

Whatever investment decisions you reach, I urge you to not only get started as soon as possible, but also to add to your investment on a regular basis.

Doing so will give you the greatest chance to insure that the powerful effects of compounding will have sufficient time to work for you, and will add significantly to your wealth.

If you do in fact select one or more of the wealth building alternatives that I have presented, and stick with that investment for the long term, I truly believe that you will be amply rewarded for your efforts. Not only will you enjoy rewards that are likely to far exceed any expectations that you may have previously held, but also an opportunity for an early or enhanced retirement will be well within your reach.

Retire Early, Retire Well

Works Cited

Books:

The Cash Book. Louisiana: Jefferson Research, 1992.
Gaffe, Austin J. Fundamentals of Real Estate. New
Jersey: Prentice-Hall, 1989.

Hicks, Tyler G. How to Make Big Money in Real Estate
in the Tighter, Tougher '90s Market. Englewood Cliffs:
Prentice-Hall, 1992.

Snowden, Richard W. Buying a Business. New York:
AMACOM, 1993.

Current Biography Yearbook. Graham. 53rd. Ed.
New York. Wilson, 1992.

Band, Richard E. Financial Independence. Potomac:
Profitable Investing, 1992.

Pamphlet/Reports:
Are you among the 76 million Americans who aren't
saving enough for retirement? New York, Merrill
Lynch, Pierce, Fenner & Smith, 1993.

<u>Piper Report</u>, Roger Casey & Associates Inc., C. J. Lawrence prospectus. 1993.

<u>Piper Report</u>, Roger Casey & Associates Inc., C. J. Lawrence prospectus. Jan 95.

<u>Access Report</u>, Dean Witter Reynolds Inc., Dec 92 and Dec 94.

<u>Money Manager Review</u>, 1993 Spring Issue. Vol. XXI, Brandes Investment Partners, Inc. prospectus Jan 93.

<u>Magazines</u>:

Welles, Edward 0. "How to Get Rich in America." <u>Inc</u>. Jan. 1993: 50-56.

Kirkpatrick, David. "Managing: Ideas & Solutions." <u>Fortune</u> Dec. 1995: 220.

Newspapers:

Gould, Carols. "Pension tension," With retirement more difficult than ever, financial pros advise a mix of investments." <u>San Diego Union-Tribune</u> 6 Sept. 1993: C-2.

Clement, Jonathan. "Why It's Risky Not to Invest More in Stocks." <u>Wall Street Journal</u> 10 Feb. 1992: C-1+.

Quinn, Jane Bryant. "Diversified stock holdings should be part of the plan." <u>San Diego Union-Tribune</u> 8 May 1996: C-3.

O'Shoughnessy, Lynn. "Unemployed workers finding success in service sector." <u>San Diego Union-Tribune</u> 25 Jan. 1994: section two 13+.

Steinmetz, Greg. Sinconolfi, Michael. "Chips off the Rock." <u>Wall Street Journal</u>, Western Ed. 1 Dec. 1993: A-1+.

Bauder, Don. "Were dealt Prudential for client?" San <u>Diego Union-Tribune</u> 24 Jan. 1993:1-3.

Newsletters:

<u>Mutual Fund Forecaster</u>. Fort Lauderdale: The Institute for Econometrics Research, Jan. 1992.

<u>Straight Talk on Your Money</u>. Potomac: Phillips Oct. 1993; Nov. 1993.

<u>Louis Rukeyser's Wall Street</u>. Alexandria: Rukeyser, Feb. 1994.

OTHER RESOURCES

Books:

O'Higgins, Michael. Beating the Dow. New York: Harper Collins, 1991

Lynch, Peter. One up on Wall Street. New York: Simon & Shuster, 1989

Ester, Jack. Compound Interest and Annuity Tables. New York: McGraw Hill paperbacks. 1976

Brouner, Dennis. Investing In Real Estate: How To Do It Right. Chicago: Longman Financial Services, 1986

Haight, Timothy & Singer, Daniel. The Real Estate Investment Advisor. Chicago: Probus, 1988/91

Monthly Interest Amortization Tables, Chicago: Contemporary Books, 1984 Kishel, Gregory & Patricia.

How to Start, Run and Stay in Business. New York: John Wiley & Sons, 1993

Dailey, Gene. Secrets Of A Successful Entrepreneur. Pleasonton: K & A Publications, 1993

Newsletters:

<u>Beating the Dow.</u> The Hirsch Organization Inc., Six Dear Trail, Old Tappan, N.J. 07675

Mark Skousen's <u>Forecast & Strategies</u>. Phillips Publishing Inc., 7811 Montrose Rd., Potomac, MD 20854

<u>Fabian's Investment Resource</u>. P.O. Box 2538 Huntington Beach, CA 92647

INDEX